STILL ME...
After All These Years

STILL ME...

After All These Years

24 Writers Reflect on Aging

KAREN HELENE WALKER

Still Me...After All These Years

ISBN-13: 978-1542894357
ISBN-10: 1542894352

Book Design / Consulting Editor: Mark David Gerson
www.markdavidgerson.com

Cover / Author Photograph: Kathleen Messmer
www.kathleenmessmer.com

Also By Karen Helene Walker

• *The Wishing Steps*

• *Following the Whispers: Creating a Life of Inner Peace and Self-Acceptance from the Depths of Despair*

• *Singing My Soul (Coming Soon!)*

Age is a limit we impose upon ourselves.
"Lost Horizon," screenplay by Robert Riskin

For my friends Aaron and Ellie Gordon,
who continue to inspire me as I move
through this process of aging.

Contents

Preface

SOME TIME AGO, my friend Ellie Gordon surprised me by saying, "I don't see 'me' anymore when I look in the mirror."

"Who do you see?" I asked.

"An old lady who walks with a walker or a cane." Ellie was then eighty-eight.

"But, you're still you. The walker doesn't define you."

"I know. But it's the first thing others see," she said.

I couldn't stop thinking about that conversation, especially as I have been contemplating writing something on aging for the past ten years. You see, I'm a sixty-something baby boomer who cared for both my dad and my mother-in-law. I also helped two older friends who have since passed away. My friends and I have had many discussions about growing older and dying and about how we want to move through this process with grace and dignity. But other projects always took precedence, and I never got clarity on what this aging project should be.

Then, while on a writing retreat with my friend Wendy Brown, inspiration struck: Why not make this an anthology? How much wiser and richer it could be if others were to share their experiences of this journey called aging. If they were to share about the challenges and opportunities that come when you reach that point in life where mortality is a more imminent reality. About how aging changes you, or doesn't. How it impacts your life, both positively and negatively. Does your way of thinking change? What about your behavior? Have your priorities shifted? Do you think about dying? Do you hate the way you look? That conversation with Ellie led to the title and theme of this anthology: *Still Me...After All These Years.*

When we're young, we think we are invincible. We can't imagine growing old. But something happens after we turn fifty or sixty, especially if we lose someone we love. We realize how impermanent life is and that someday we'll be gone. But before we die, we have to accept and deal with growing older — old age. Many of us first become acquainted with old age when we begin dealing with aging parents. But whenever and wherever we are when the aging process begins for us, there is one thing we know for sure: At some point we are going to die, and we usually don't know when or how. It comes when it comes. How we deal with the journey is what this collection is all about.

Buddhism teaches that to live with intention and right consciousness, one must be aware of death. Native American culture teaches about the cycles of life, birth/death, the seasons. I'm sure there are parts of American culture that address death and dying, but it seems to me that mostly we deny death. Our paradigm is to stay as young as we can for as long as we can and then put ourselves out to pasture until we die.

I'm not one who thought about death much. I don't think I'm afraid of it. But I am afraid of getting old. I've seen what happens. Some lose their ability to think clearly; some can't walk as far or as well; others lose their words, their friends, their family members and pieces of themselves. Things we loved to do — like hiking, needlepoint, singing, dancing, reading, driving — disappear like melting snow.

Elders tell me they wonder why they are still here. What is their purpose? I found myself replying, "Why do you need a purpose? Isn't it enough that you are you? You are a gift, whether or not you can still do the things you used to do." Easy for me to say. I'm not quite at that stage yet.

Do you want to know what it's really like? Within these pages, you will find essays and poems from folks ranging in age from sixty to ninety. People from different races, different religions and varied professional backgrounds have all shared their personal stories about aging. Whether you relate to the specifics of their stories or not, hopefully you'll find a kernel of wisdom to fortify you during your journey toward aging.

Karen Helene Walker
March 2017

It's Never Too Late to Follow Your Dreams

MARK DAVID GERSON

"The important thing to you is not how many years in your life, but how much life in your years!"

EDWARD J. STIEGLITZ

I TURNED SIXTY-TWO a few weeks ago, making me a few months older than my mother when she died and six years older than my father when he passed away. In less than two weeks, I will visit my urologist with the full expectation that he will order a prostate biopsy, my third biopsy in as many years. Given the post-election uncertainty that exists at this writing around Obamacare, which provided me with my first health insurance in nearly two decades, it is impossible to know what my options will be should the biopsy reveal a problem or, even if it doesn't, whether it will be possible for that potential problem to be monitored in years to come.

I don't share this here in order to paint a poor-me, doom-and-gloom scenario. I always do my best to remain positive in the face of life's vicissitudes, and I am certain that things will work out for the best for me, whatever that turns out to mean. Rather, I share it because although I am not old by twenty-first-century standards, aging brings with it certain risks, whoever we are. Whoever we are, those same risks also offer opportunities. Perhaps one of the most powerful is the gift of focus.

When my mother was sixty-one, not long after she was diagnosed with cancer, she and

I were sitting together on her living floor one evening, our only light the sickly sodium-vapor yellow filtering in through the venetian blinds from the street light outside. I had been over for my weekly dinner and Scrabble game and we were waiting for my stepfather to return from a class so he could drive me to the subway.

By then chemotherapy had thinned my mother's thick hair into baby silk. Her wig, which matched the dark brown coloring she had been applying since the first strands of gray began to show up years earlier, sat pinned to its stand in her bedroom. She no longer wore it around the house. Her pride in her appearance had weakened. Or perhaps she had grudgingly surrendered to the fact that she could no longer control her appearance...or much of anything else.

I can't remember now whether she looked at me or away as she spoke into the silence. "I've made a lot of poor choices in my life," she said softly.

It felt then as though she was referring to both her marriages. Each had been con-venient; neither ever seemed to bring her much joy. With stereotypical Jewish-mother guilt, she may also have been holding herself responsible for my homosexuality, my sister's teen rebelliousness and all other perceived deficiencies in our lives — past, present and future. And what unrealized dreams had she been carrying through her sixty years that now, because of those choices and her health, seemed unattainable?

More than three decades later, that scene still haunts me. I wonder today whether those ten words, spoken as much to herself as to me, indicated that she had already stopped fighting for her life. Was she just going through the motions with her chemo and radiation treatments? Was she simply doing what was expected of her, as she had done for most of her life? I will never know. All I know is that she was dead little more than a year later.

If at age twenty-nine, I couldn't grasp my mother's despair, it has become easier to understand as I, too, now have more years to look back on than I am likely to have to look forward to.

That incontrovertible fact branded itself onto my awareness three years ago, when, in the months after Obamacare made it possible for me to have long-overdue routine medical tests, various body parts indicated that they were functioning less than optimally, in some cases with potentially terminal implications.

Unlike my mother, who at some level may have viewed her cancer diagnosis as a welcome "way out," I chose to view what seemed like a never ending cascade of alarming news as an opportunity. Not that I wasn't terrified. I was. Much of the time.

One day, however, when I wasn't consumed by panic, I asked the question many of us of a certain age find ourselves asking, even without medical prompting: "If I'm to die sooner rather than later, what is it that I want to make sure I do before I go?" Before I had even finished formulating the question in my mind, the answer that surged into my conscious awareness was "write another novel."

I have been a writer for a long time — writing fiction, memoir, inspiration and books for writers. Through that time, I have rarely known in advance what the books I begin will be about. And so when, soon after, I started to write this unexpected and unplanned "bucket list" novel, I had no idea what it would be about or where it would take me. Imagine my surprise when the theme that emerged in *Sara's Year*, a story loosely based on my mother's, turned out to be "it's never too late to follow your dreams."

In the story, the death, with her passions unrealized, of the title character's oldest friend triggers a series of events that reignites Sara's long-abandoned aspiration to be a writer. She publishes her first book at age sixty-four and discovers what her friend Esther could not, that it's never to late to follow your dreams.

That's what I meant back at the start of this essay about the gift of focus. Sometimes, we need a little shove to point us toward our dreams. For Sara, it took Esther's death. For my creation of Sara, it took a forceful reminder of my mortality.

It is easy to assume, as Esther and my mother may have done, that aging is a death sentence that renders our hopes and dreams irrelevant. It's just not true. It's never too late to follow your dreams.

In researching a talk I gave recently on dreams and aging, I was reminded that Grandma Moses did not start painting seriously until she was seventy-eight. I also discovered Betty Lindberg of Atlanta, a self-described couch potato who went on her first run at sixty-three and set a new world record at ninety-one. Then there's Norma Jean Bauerschmidt. Diagnosed with stage-four uterine cancer at ninety, she chose to forgo treatment and instead took an epic, cross-country road trip with her son and daughter-in-law.

It's never too late to follow your dreams.

None of us can know what the future holds for us. All we can know is that its duration in this physical form is limited. I can't, for example, know whether my urologist will order another prostate biopsy and if he does, what the implications and consequences will be, with or without health insurance. Nor can I know whether some other condition, age-related or otherwise, will show up to frighten me today, tomorrow, next month or next year. All I know is that I have more books to write, including a new one that I plan to start work on tomorrow, and more dreams to discover and fulfill. All I know is that it's never too late to follow my dreams.

Who Needs a Facelift?

Valerie Capps

*"Considering the alternative,
it's not too bad at all."*

Maurice Chevalier (on aging)

REMEMBER WHEN WE BABY boomers didn't trust anyone over thirty? I suppose we never imagined we would eventually be thirty-something ourselves. Back then it never even occurred to me that one day I would be on the downside of sixty, but here I am, "a baby boomer senior citizen." Is that an oxymoron?

One evening last year I looked in the mirror and wondered: Where did the years go, and who is that stranger looking back at me?

When the wrinkles were faint, I didn't mind them so much. I simply used a lot of concealers, slathered on the latest beauty cream and convinced myself that they weren't that noticeable.

When my hair started turning gray, my hairdresser merely covered the gray with a darker color. I cut my hair into one of the over-sixty bob styles that are acceptable for mature women. Someone made an unspoken rule many years ago that said women over a certain age can't wear their hair long unless tucked into a tidy bun.

I hid those extra pounds I'd piled on over the previous couple of decades with dark colors and a looser fit. My hemline gradually dropped lower and eventually I found my closet filled with elastic-waist pants and baggie tops.

Last year my husband and I took a cruise

with friends of his whom I had never met. We were three couples. I was the youngest woman, but I soon realized I looked the oldest.

I haven't had on a bathing suit for over twenty years, but both my new female friends unself-consciously showed up at the beach in their modest but flattering suits. I self-consciously wore my capris and an oversized T-shirt into the clear, blue waters of the Caribbean.

That first evening at dinner, I noticed how good one of the women's faces looked and asked which skincare and makeup line she used. She smiled and told me it was a facelift, not makeup.

I was surprised. When I thought of facelifts, what came to mind were visions of star-tled-looking women with wrinkly necks or the bad results I'd noticed on certain aging celebrities, not this vibrant sixty-nine-year-old who could pass for a mid-fifties jet-setter.

The mirror officially became my enemy that day. I can't remember the last time I had taken a long, hard look at myself. Standing in front of the full-length mirror in our cabin, I saw an overweight matronly woman looking back at me. Where had the real me gone? When had she left?

"Do I look old and fat?" I asked my husband, who never lies to me.

"Do I look stupid?" he asked back.

That was it! Time to make a change. We returned home on Sunday, and on Monday

I called to make an appointment with a respected, *licensed* plastic surgeon. I'd read somewhere Priscilla Presley went to an unlicensed phony for her facelift. Not me, thank you very much.

The consultation went well. The doctor explained the whole procedure, and I told him I didn't want to look like a plastic Barbie when it was over. He agreed, said I was a good candidate and added that I'd be pleased with the subtle results.

Next came a meeting with the appointment scheduler and an estimation of costs. (No, Medicare doesn't pay anything for this type of surgery. Nothing. Nada.) When I got the estimate, I slapped my hand on my chest and thought about asking for a cardiologist to help me get over the shock!

I don't know what I was thinking. Four to six thousand dollars, perhaps? I hadn't given much thought to the price, but I certainly hadn't expected the bill to be near twelve thousand dollars!

My husband and I are both retired. We aren't destitute, but neither are we flush. Let's just say that if I spent that much money on my appearance, there wouldn't be anything left to take that face out anywhere to show it off.

My husband and I didn't even discuss the options. I made the decision alone. No-way, no-how would I spend that much of our savings for vanity's sake. I already have a difficult time

29

justifying the purchase of new clothes now that I'm no longer working.

I was a little disheartened for a couple of days, then I realized that in the scheme of things, this was way down on my list of life's disappointments.

A facelift to make me look and feel better was out of reach, but maybe I could make other changes that would give me a reason to get up every morning and face myself in the mirror.

While mulling over the current state of my life, I remembered that I had spent most of my working days wishing for more time to devote to my first love, writing. I suddenly realized that while I now had that extra time, I had been wasting the opportunity. A new resolution was born: I would get up every morning and write something. Anything.

Currently, I have completed four short-story Kindle books that are available on Amazon. I also write a weekly blog and have ghost-written and sold several articles and two other ebooks.

Next came the weight issue. My doctor had been telling me for years to lose weight and lower my cholesterol. I'd made half-hearted attempts but nothing serious. I promptly made another resolution, to eat better and exercise (walk) more. No strict diet, no goal of a significant weight loss, merely a change in my lifestyle. I've lost eight pounds, but more important than the weight loss is the fact that I feel better...healthier.

Now for the hair. I told my hairdresser I wanted something different. I didn't want a style for a twenty-something girl, but I wanted a change. I let my hair grow a little; got a softer cut; had it highlighted.

Last came the wardrobe. I'm retired so I don't need a lot of clothes. Comfort clothes are fine for writing on my laptop at home, and I have a lot of those. But I needed a few things to wear out in public.

Instead of buying oversized tops and polyester stretch pants, I opted for a nicely fitted pair of black slacks, a pair of NYDJ (Not Your Daughter's Jeans) and a couple of flattering tops and dresses. I justified it to myself with the one dress/pant size I'd dropped. I have had foot surgery, so stilettos are out. But I invested in a pair of comfortable ballet flats that go with just about everything. I also bought a new bathing suit for our next vacation! Total cost: about five hundred dollars.

What about the plastic surgery? I've come to accept that, for me at least, the best and least expensive natural facelift I can get is a smile that reaches my eyes. Sure, there are a few wrinkles involved, but what the heck? People don't seem to notice the visible flaws if you have a friendly smile on your face.

Recently, people have asked me if I've had work done. When I say no, they tell me that I look different. Some say I look ten years younger. I don't know about that, but I certainly feel better than I have in years, and the price was very reasonable.

Somewhere between the weight loss and the new hairstyle, I decided that I'm okay with me. I have come to realize I'd rather spend money making memories traveling than trying to regain my lost youth.

I've decided that I'll simply have to do my best to grow old gracefully and trust that in the years to come, people will take a moment to look past my aging facade and discover the true essence of a wrinkled, but contented old woman.

Walking Toward

LINDA HOYE

"How old would you be if you didn't know how old you are?"

SATCHEL PAIGE

THREE YEARS AGO I walked away. I left behind the pressures of a corporate career where I managed projects with deadlines that seemed impossible, implemented directives that made no sense and tried to convince my team that we were doing the right thing. I felt like I was at the top of my game. I was bringing in a six-figure income that provided both a good measure of security and the opportunity to spend money mindlessly to soothe the stress that was my constant and faithful companion. I was fulfilled in my work but also in the sense that I was too busy to have time to think.

A restlessness had settled over me a few years earlier, a resentment that the best of me was being given to a corporation while my core self was starved from inattention. The key, I told someone during those restless years, was not to walk away from something, but to walk toward something. I saw the something I wanted to walk toward as clear as the Canadian sky on a sunny summer afternoon. I made a plan, set a course and started walking toward it.

I was fifty-five years old on that Friday in February when I left the office for the last time, carrying a massive bouquet of fifty-five long-stemmed roses that my husband had delivered earlier in the week in honor of my retirement-eligible birthday. After all the months of planning and preparation, sleepless nights and cranky days, that final day — handing over my security badge, making one last round to say goodbye, gathering my things and walking out — seemed anticlimactic.

My mom, who died suddenly at age fifty-five, was the beacon I followed as I walked through the doors that afternoon. Her death when I was a young woman in my twenties had been the catalyst I needed to change my life, propelling me to go back to school, leave an abusive marriage and become the strong, capable woman I had forgotten I could be. Her dying became my living. It also set within me an awareness of how the whisper of a life can be silenced in an instant, and I resolved to retire as soon as I could, lest I die selling my soul to a corporation while forgetting to live. Mom had been gone for thirty years but she was still guiding me as I ascended the cement stairs leading toward the parking lot.

My steps felt light with anticipation. I was finally free. I had made it.

All of our plans were coming together. The list of tasks required for us to repatriate to Canada, a list that had once seemed insurmountable, had been whittled down to a manageable few. Our house in Washington State was empty, save for an air mattress and the few necessities we needed for one final night's stay. The paperwork we needed to have with us when we crossed the border was organized and ready to go. A new home in a modest fifty-five-plus community, and a new life in Canada, awaited. I felt like I had jumped off the side of a cliff and was free-falling — exhilarated and terrified at the same time.

I was physically exhausted as we unpacked, organized and settled into our new home, emotionally spent as I began to wind down from the pace of getting it all done. I slept well for the first time in many years. Months went by and I continued to sleep through the night and wake refreshed in the morning. Gone were the sleepless nights spent worrying about projects. Gone were the mornings when I hit the snooze button three times before forcing myself to rise. I realized this was my new normal.

I felt guilty when someone asked what I did for a living, and I grew weary of hearing, "Oh, but you're so young," when I confessed my retired state. One person's young had been my mom's end of the road. I wasn't young. I was living on borrowed time.

I wondered, for a time, who I was now that I wasn't a Business Analyst. Should I call myself Writer? Photographer? Gardener? Couldn't I just be Me? Could that be enough?

I got used to occasional sharp intakes of breath, and moments of panic, when I remembered we were living without the safety net of a corporate paycheck. I obsessed over spreadsheets and accounts. We had planned and saved, and our financial advisor assured us we were prepared. But still...

I pushed myself and set deadlines as I began new projects and set new priorities. I worked at home and in my garden with the same driven pace I had done for the corporation, seeking significance, still, in doing. Gone were house-keepers who once cared for my home. It was my job now and, with the help of a willing husband who vacuumed weekly and cleaned the toilets, I embraced it and began to inhabit, and manage, our home in a way I hadn't for years.

It took a while, longer than I expected, but in time thoughts of my old life began to fade and I started to relax and feel that the post-ca-reer me still had something to offer. I even began allowing myself permission to let go and just be now and then.

I'm thankful for the blessing of the simple life I live today. In the summertime I tend my garden and preserve the bounty; in the winter I embrace the Danish concept of *hygge* and settle into the cozy months with books and hot tea. I take photographs, and study to learn new things. I write, and learn new things about myself in the process of wrangling words and sentences. I have coffee or lunch with friends; my husband and I take short trips now and then; our grand-daughter comes to spend a week with us a few times a year. It's a good and satisfying life.

The corporate career track was a good trip and I'm glad to have taken it. I'm equally glad that it's over. The journey made me a stronger and wiser woman; it taught me what is important and what's worth letting go of. I've come full circle now, and renewed my acquaintance with the woman I was as a young adult. We don't always see eye-to-eye, but I've come to appreciate her idiosyncrasies.

Now, three years after that day when I walked out, I'm approaching the age that my other mother — my birth mother — was when she died suddenly; coincidentally, also from a pulmonary embolism. I can't help but wonder if this is also to be my destiny. I find myself wondering if I have done enough, and if I have been enough. These are the things I think about on those rare nights when I lay awake.

I continue down a path that is ever changing and fraught with reminders that my time here is fleeting. A body that is changing, news of illness, sudden deaths: These things all remind me that one day I'll move on from here. After my mom died I chose to change the trajectory of my life; I did it again when I walked away from corporate life. With the same intentionality, I make choices daily that shape the legacy I will leave behind when my time here is over.

I walk on; and I walk toward.

On Being a Woman of a Certain Age

KAREN HELENE WALKER

"There is a fountain of youth: it is your mind, your talents, the creativity you bring to your life and the lives of the people you love. When you learn to tap this source, you will have truly defeated age."

SOPHIA LOREN

Ahhhh! Do that again. *Ahhhh!*

Yes, that's right. Heave a big sigh.
You deserve it. You've worked hard. You can rest now.

Breathe.
Breathe in that you've made it thus far.
Breathe in that you've gained much wisdom.
Breathe in that you can do what you want.

You know who you are.
You know what hurts and how to fix it, or where to find help if you don't.

Breathe. Let go. Surrender.

Not happy with your looks?
When will you let go of trying to please others?
Isn't it time to just feel good about you?

Got wrinkles?
Embrace them. They are the tracks of your life.

Do you sag?
Those are body parts resting after their long journey. Let them rest.

You're done doing. No more expectations. Only desires.

Let your heart dream and know you have the wisdom to follow. Or not.

It's a choice, not a should.

Your soul knows what it wants and needs to age gracefully.

Listen. Ask questions. Hear the answers.

Whatever lessons still need learning, know you will learn them.

Your age is just a number. What's important is to embrace who you've become.

Now.
At this age.

Not who you were at twenty or thirty or even forty.

Allow.
Accept.
Acknowledge.
Adjust.
Absolve.
Adore.

Ahhhh! Do that again. *Ahhhh!*

Dependence and Independence

ELLIE GORDON

"The afternoon knows what the morning never suspected."

ROBERT FROST

THERE ARE TWO TERMS that occur to me which could be my framework for aging: dependence and independence.

With aging, it seems inevitable that people generally follow one of these two paths. My path of independence is the outcome of living a life that has given me comfort and security without any thought about the future. When I was younger, the future was always far enough ahead so that I didn't have to think about it. The independent path, I think, more realistically prepares one for an unknown future that could include health issues, loss of a mate, perhaps a reduction in income. And hopefully, tools to deal with whatever might show up.

I now live in a facility where I can usually see who falls into these categories. Many women are indecisive, uncertain and fearful. These women fall into what I call the dependent category. On the other hand, I also see people who are more self-sufficient and have a sense of who they are and how they fit into this environment. They seem to want to hold onto much of their independence. When I moved into this facility I had to find out for myself how I fit in.

My interests are different from those of many of the residents who live here, so I've had to find my own niche; when it didn't exist, I created my own. For example, I formed a small committee of residents whose mission is to examine and change policies to better meet residents' needs. I also created a music appreciation event which occurs bimonthly. In addition, I encouraged people to sign up and attend theater outings, which prompted the facility to begin including that event in its regularly scheduled activities. These are projects that helped me continue to express who I am and made me more comfortable with my life here.

A sense of independence catapulted me into a life I could not have imagined, in that I have had to learn to relate to different kinds of people. I have learned to be more sympathetic with other peoples' feelings and issues, and I've learned to relate to people who come from backgrounds that were once entirely foreign to me.

Aging has broadened my perspective of life, and I now find myself listening in ways I never have before. On the one hand, I have been independent in terms of my thinking and in my professional life. On the other hand, I have had, in spite of this independence, total emotional support, especially in moments of uncertainty. I've been fortunate in having both and that has served me well. Until now. Now, the reality of age and the aging process has kicked in. Because for the first time in my life, I find that I am dependent in ways I've never been dependent before. I require the assistance of my husband in ways I've never needed before. So I've had to learn a sense of dependency with a degree of grace. My feisty independence has made me fight this every step of the way. Because the reality is that that sense of feistiness, which can keep me going, can also be self-defeating.

For example, using a four-wheel walker enhances my stability and I've been told it must become my best friend. At the same time, when I go into a restaurant or theater lobby or participate in a social situation, I wish I could leave my best friend home because it seems to create in my mind a persona that I don't like.

I've had to learn a whole new set of coping skills as a result of the changes in my life. And I had to be willing to accept these changes. That hasn't been easy. I went from looking in the mirror and not knowing who I was to looking in the mirror and accepting the person I see there. Because of a condition in my right eye that I refuse to admit will be permanent (an example of my feistiness), I have had to learn to read on a Kindle, which has been a blessing because you don't have to schlep a big book around with you. But it's also been a curse because I've had to give up the pleasure of holding and touching the pages of the real books I have loved my whole life.

Perhaps the most challenging change

that aging has created is in my marriage. As these kinds of life changes happen, I find that internal changes also need to take place. My husband and I have realized that we need to constantly stay in touch because each new life-style change creates a new conversation.

We've tried, as successfully as we can, to deal with new and challenging circumstances. That has become a full-time job. Constant talking keeps my sixty-five-year-long marriage alive and vital. As I reflect on these changes, I realize that the line between independence and dependence is becoming more blurred as I approach my nineties. Is this good or not? Who knows, but it is what it is.

Ellie Gordon's eye condition may or may not be permanent, but it made it necessary for her to dictate this essay to me. – Karen Helene Walker

Aging and the Joy of Sex

PAT GARCIA

"The spirit never ages."
ISABEL ALLENDE

IT IS DRIZZLING. Not drop-by-drop but lightly against the window panes. I'm sitting alone at a corner table for four drinking my café latte in the Brussels National Airport. It is overflowing with people flying out to their different destinations and I am one of them. It is summer in Europe. Children are out of school for six weeks. Parents have packed their vans, cars or mobile trailers or have purchased airplane or cruise tickets and are taking their children on vacation. Europe has practically shut down. As for me, I am on my way to Georgia to visit my family.

The moody sky gets darker; the rain falls harder, no longer dribbling against the windows lightly but in noisy splats while I contemplate whether to desert my table to go purchase a newspaper. To have a table alone is precious because people are looking for somewhere to sit, and I know that as soon as I get up, it will be gone. If the sun were shining, everyone would be scrambling to sit outside, but the rain has crammed people into an international terminal that now seems much too small. As I ponder my options, three European women approach me and ask if they can share my table. Unlike in the US, Europeans don't have a problem sitting next to strangers in public places or sharing a table. So, having learned on this continent to share my personal space, I smile politely, say yes and ask them to watch my things while I go to the newspaper stand.

When I return, the women are talking among themselves. I do my best to concentrate on the magazine I am reading and not to eavesdrop, but their conversation intrigues me. They are talking about sexual intimacy after turning fifty. I glimpse slyly over my magazine at each woman, not wanting to believe they are that old. Casually dressed in the latest fashion, they could easily pass for early forties.

I have never given much thought to sexuality and aging. I come from the Deep South, from a family of Southern Baptist African Americans who follow the "strong-black-women syndrome" and believe that decent African American women don't need love. Instead, we give love to everyone else. As for sex, we are seen as either insatiable Jezebels or easy breeders. In either case, not much consideration is given to our sexual satisfaction.

"What do you think?" inquires the woman to my right.

"About what?" I look up guiltily, ashamed that they have caught me listening in.

"About sex after fifty."

I think about my family, and I relate to them a recent situation. When my grandfather died at seventy-one, he left my grandmother alone on their farm. A family crisis erupted when it was discovered that my grandmother had started dating a man. I viewed the situation differently than my aunts and cousins, who were extremely displeased with my grandmother's behavior. They saw my grandma as a mother and grandmother, but not as a woman who needed to have sex.

"Why do you see it differently?" the woman across from me asks.

"Why shouldn't she have a male friend?" I shoot back. "What's wrong with her receiving TLC from a man who desires her? Where in the world does it state that my granny has to be lonely?" I am defensive, but the woman has touched a tender spot. I love my grandmother and am protective of her. I call her often from Europe just to talk. "Thinking back on how I was raised," I continue, "it seems to me that my aunts and cousins are only looking at my grandmother as 'grandma' and not as a woman."

The three women look at each other. Our table is silent. Without my realizing it, my words have touched upon the real problem simmering beneath the surface.

"My family is getting on my very last nerve," the woman to my right says, "and it is pissing me off. Just because I tell them that I'm dating a younger man, they start freaking out. They don't understand that I have needs they can't fulfill."

The woman across from me joins in and begins telling her story. She says that after she raised her children, their father left her for a younger woman. Although it took her some time to recover from her feelings of abandonment, she succeeded with the help of a man twelve years younger than she is. In her children's eyes, she is sexless. They expect her to help care for and nurture her grandchildren. However, the man she is secretly dating awakens desires in her that have gone unfulfilled for years. "How do you make your children understand and accept that you want to live and experience life and not be a full-time, unpaid babysitter?" she asks before confessing that she is sneaking out with her young man, going to restaurants outside of the city and closeting herself in hotels with him where they won't be recognized.

The anguish in her voice breaks my heart. Here is a woman who is afraid of taking a chance on openly loving her new partner because she doesn't want to lose contact with her grandkids or her children.

I wish I had answers for her, but I don't. I do, however, see the irony in their situation as it relates to my own. Single, I recognize issues buried deep within me about how I handle my own sexual needs — not only now, but as I grow older.

A few minutes later, I hear the announcement over the loudspeakers that my flight will start boarding. I gather my things, say goodbye and wish the women a safe flight. But as I walk to my gate, I can't get our conversation out of my head.

I am now sixty-seven and moving toward the golden years of life, my eighties. I married at thirty-eight, three years after that airport encounter. The joy of learning, of discovering, of loving, of being sexually intimate with my partner has become an ingrained part of my life, thanks in part to my time with those three women. I experience sex to its fullest. It is integral in helping me maintain my emotional balance and my well-being.

I don't believe in coincidences. Nothing happens by chance. I was destined to meet those women on that particular day. When I think of the fact that I sat in a café in an airport crowded with people looking for places to sit and no one approached me until those three women did, it confirms my belief that we were destined to meet. I doubt that I will ever run into them again, but sharing our ideas about sex after fifty forced me to change my way of thinking and to take action about the kind of woman I wanted to be. I can honestly say that I am a different woman today because of our encounter. It ignited a chain reaction that changed my future.

In the months that followed, I started discovering who I was as a woman, as a sexual being, and what my desires were. I asked myself what would it take for me to be sexually active as long as I wanted to be. The questions were not easy to face and answer, but I did not shun them. I challenged myself to meet the requirements to keep my body physically fit and maintain a certain level of nimbleness. I started mentally exercising my brain by learning new things and most importantly, I removed the age barrier that we adults tend to raise that keeps us from associating with people younger than ourselves, and I opened myself up to learn from them. Connecting with people younger than I am stimulates the child in me and keeps me fresh, alive and adventuresome.

What will I do when and if I reach eighty? I don't know. The future is unpredictable. I can't even tell you what will happen if my husband dies before I do. Will I change my mind and stop practicing sexual intimacy? At this moment, I don't think so. I do not believe age or the death of a partner should dictate whether a person should or should not be intimately engaged in intercourse. I learned that from the experiences my grandmother and I shared together. She is an inspiration as to how a person can enjoy life as long as he or she lives.

Sexuality is a part of life. Connecting physically with a partner generates warmth, joy and compassion. It goes beyond procreating and increasing the population; it is a God-given pleasure. For me, that means that growing older is not about preparing myself for the grave. It is not the end of experiencing sexual enjoyment. Rather, it is the continuation of a lifelong journey, if I wish it to be.

If not for those three women in the Brussels airport those many years ago, I don't believe that I would have made a commitment to discover me and what I am all about. Our conversation influenced my life and for that I am extremely grateful. Sexual intimacy never grows old and never dies. It remains forever a part of us. After all, isn't making love with our partners for as long as physically possible one of the most enjoyable pleasures and greatest gifts given to humans?

I Don't Really Mind Aging. Well, Maybe a Little!

KATHLEEN MESSMER

"Wrinkles should merely indicate where smiles have been."

MARK TWAIN

So HERE'S THE THING: I remember sitting on the hood of a '57 Oldsmobile convertible when I was seventeen with my then-boyfriend and him playing with my straight, waist-length hair and me feeling very skittish. It didn't progress much past that because I was a "good girl." Damn it! It all worked out, though, because I did end up marrying him later, and I have a wonderful son from that very brief union.

When I look back on that, I just shake my head and smile. I was sure I had it all figured out then. I didn't, of course, but I sure thought I did. Life went on and thirteen years later I was on marriage number three and had another amazing son.

Here's what I've learned (maybe) since then. I still feel like a youngster, mostly. In my mind, at least, I am wiser. I'm not even close to being as shapely (annoying, for sure, since I used to be a personal trainer!). And I wish I knew then what I know now, because my life would have been very different. It hasn't been terrible. Not by a long shot. Not like some folks. But it could have been more comfortable, less stressful and had fewer struggles, and I could have probably done without so many friggin' husbands.

I'm a filmmaker and photographer, and my age doesn't really stop me from doing anything

I want to do, but I can definitely feel it some days — especially once we hit the twelve-hour-plus mark on set. I work out six days a week, and it takes me longer to recover from most aches and pains, but I try not to let that slow me down too much. It must be that stubborn German-Irish-English stock I hail from.

All that said, when I look in the mirror these days, I do still see me, just a more robust, pebbly, droopy and wrinkly version. I often wonder *how* that happened and who the hell is that staring back at me? My only consolation is that every once in a while I get carded and it makes my day! The person who cards me always gets a *huge* tip.

I haven't really experienced ageism, but I have experienced sexism. The pat on the head... the "little lady" comments...the smiles that say "let it go"...the "is it that time of month?" remarks. It's truly infuriating. I realize I grew up in a generation that put up with that crap, but I don't. Not ever. Not anymore. It's disrespectful and I don't take that from anyone. Especially at my age.

I have to say, though, that when I went back to my hometown for my fortieth high school reunion a few years back, I was floored at how really bad a lot of my classmates looked. Especially the ones who were the popular kids back in the day. (Oops! Did I say that out loud?) Since then, they seem to be dropping like flies and I keep thinking, "But they're my age! This is way too young to die." I guess I have lived and continue to live better than most — health-wise, physically and mentally. I try to always maintain a generally positive outlook because being otherwise is not acceptable to me, not by any stretch of the imagination. I keep telling my kids I plan to live until I'm a hundred and twenty, at least. They look at me and say, "Oh, my God! We have to wait that long for our money?" I reply, "No, it'll all be gone by then!"

I went back to school when I was forty-six, the result of a work injury; I had to go back in order to maintain my disability. Not my idea of fun, but here's what happened: I loved it! So much so that I just kept going. I got my under-grad degree the same year my youngest son graduated high school. Weird, right? It was the year of graduations, for sure. I took a three-year break, then decided to go to grad school. At fifty-three I applied, was accepted and went back to school...again. I had a blast! It took me another four years, but I did it. Got my Masters at fifty-seven and started yet another career. My kids thought I was insane, but I was having fun. I told them, "I've done you, now it's time to do me." And I did. And I still am.

The things I've discovered about myself as I've gotten older are many, and while I've always been considered "feisty," "mouthy" and "independent" (much to my mother's chagrin), there are some things that I'm relatively sure will not change any time soon. They are:

• I'm more motivated to get things done because time is rushing on and doesn't stand still for anyone or anything.

• I have less and less patience for myself or anyone else. Things need to get done and I need to be on top of it. (No control issues there!) If I'm annoyed, I let whoever is on the receiving end know it and I don't feel bad about it. "Just handle it already!"

• I want to see the world. I never had any desire before, but now that I'm a "real" photographer, it beckons me like nothing else I've ever experienced. And finally,

• I did a pretty good job at being a parent. I'm only now realizing that my boys have turned into really decent human beings. I'm proud of that beyond anything else I've ever done in my life. That is and continues to be my praoudest accomplishment. More than making movies and creating photography. More than anything.

All in all, I don't really mind aging...much. Well, maybe a little. It's a natural process that we all experience, if we're fortunate enough to live through it. I just really dislike all the resulting lines, bumps, gray hairs, widening of the derriere and general slowing down that happens. Not fair. Not fair at all!

Age: "X" Marks the Spot

Jill Plaman

"I'm not afraid of what's called age. The only thing that would ever frighten me would be losing my vitality or energy or the stars in my eyes or love for life. And I don't believe that's connected with numbers."

Dyan Cannon

AGE: AT FIRST GLANCE, a simple three-letter word and precise mathematical concept. But age, in my opinion, is more contextually, culturally and emotionally laden than almost any other three-letter word in the English language, with the exception of the word and concept of "God." It's no wonder that I, like many of us, have struggled to come to terms with its meaning throughout my life. At various times, for example...

- What does it mean to me or to others to "act my age"?

- How is age-appropriate action determined anyway? By whom? For whom?

- Do I need to act or dress differently now that I'm officially a grandmother?

By the time society has defined me as a senior citizen, my life has been "age-controlled" by a variety of external rules and mandates over which I have had no input. Society says I can start my formal education at age five, drive at sixteen, marry and vote at eighteen, drink at twenty-one, collect early social security at sixty-two and fully retire at sixty-five. Religion tells me when I can be a full-fledged member of a congregation, and the legal system has legislated when I am no longer considered a juvenile and, as an adult, can legally give consent.

Despite these myriad of imposed numerical milestones in every context of my outward life, it is how I perceive my own internal aging process and how others may see me or define me that has created the most dissonance in my life.

I have never thought of my age as a number, especially as I have grown older and have passed many, if not most of those age-related milestones. During different times in my life, I have felt both "older than my years" and "younger than my years." As a child I've been told that I'm "very mature" for my age. And as an adult, people have said I don't "look" my age. I don't identity with my numerical age as a concrete, defining attribute because I feel that it doesn't really shed much light on who I truly am. Personally, I consider age to be a state of being and level of attainment which is difficult to express adequately in a paragraph of words much less specific digits. Maybe that's why if you ask me my age, I wonder why you want to know. Do you think it will tell you something important about me? Even more importantly, do you think that the nature of our relationship should be influenced by a particular number?

Increasingly, aging has been an ever more active process for me rather than an "event" established by artificial boundaries like birthdays. The problem is that the older I get, the faster I age, and with the exception of cytogenetic freezing, there is no way to slow it down. I never liked the cold much anyway. As Einstein discovered, time is relative, and the older I am the more it relatively speeds up within me.

It's been said that youth is wasted on the young. I get that now like never before. When you are young it seems like you've been young forever and will be forever young. You don't know what you don't know and you can't experience what it is like to be over a century in age. When you get much older, you wonder what the heck happened and why you weren't there for it. It reminds me of the Carrie Fisher interview when she was talking about her last role, as the well-seasoned General Leia in the latest *Star Wars* movie; you may recall that she appeared as the youthful Princess Leia in previous movies. She wryly complained about her latest image on the big screen with her gray hair and wrinkled features saying, "Nobody told me I got old." It seems like each of us is the last to know.

Old age comes at a bad time, according to the University of Exeter's Susan Banducci. Just as my mind is expanding and I have more wisdom and positive qualities to share with the world, my personal physical world is starting to slowly but steadily diminish. My eyes don't see as well, my bones are weaker and my muscles are quicker to cramp and strain. But as a result of my lifelong experiences and struggles, I am more compassionate and more understanding toward my fellow man. The blessings that the aging process have given me are gifts I can share with others. And while I may have more to share of value, I realize I also have less time in which to do so. Therefore, I increasingly feel more compelled to actively seek opportunities to make a positive impact in other people's lives, while I can and in whatever way I can.

My mother saved, shared and lived a favorite poem of hers called "One Hundred Years From Now," author unknown. It basically said that we will not be remembered for all the wonderful things we have accumulated but we will be remembered if we were important in the life of a child. Although she passed away in 2011, she continues to be my inspiration for aging gracefully.

Some of my most jarring revelations about aging come when I compare myself to my mother at the same age. As I nostalgically look through the old family picture album, I vividly remember those times and my impressions of her. With her gray hair, wrinkles and serene smile, she seemed so old and wise. As I look at the date of the photo, calculate her age and do the math, it hits me like a lightning bolt of reality: I have now surpassed her in age! I am absolutely amazed because I don't feel the same age as I thought she looked in the picture. This is a personal, striking example of one of my most disconcerting discoveries about age and our connection to ourselves and others: Age is in the eye of the beholder. As I continue to age, "old" isn't what it used to be. Somehow old or "really old" keeps moving farther into the distance.

The most frustrating thing about aging to me is this inverse relationship of our inner (mind and spirit) bodies and our outer bodies. If age were a letter of the alphabet, it would be symbolized by the letter X with one diagonal line pointed upward and the other diagonal line pointed downward. Just as our emotional, spiritual and mental abilities continue to go upward, our physical capabilities go in the opposite direction, crossing somewhere in the middle during the course of our lives. It seems like such a shame to have this oppositional relationship of mind and body. Couldn't we just get along and grow together?

For many of us who are fortunate to live past our middle age, our inner state continues to become an ever-more-beautiful blossoming flower with thousands of outward-reaching vibrant petals, while our physical frame continues to fade, wither and sag. The spirit is at its strongest (and becoming stronger) while the body is continuing to become weaker. I believe that this is at the crux of the problem of the aging process for many of us. Perhaps that's why Bette Davis has so often been quoted as saying that "getting old ain't no place for sissies." And, in my opinion, the scariest possibility of aging is any type of diminution of our mental faculties. When I forget something, I can't help but wonder if it's just a function of my busy life or if it's the start of something more.

Perhaps some of the dissonance and ambivalence I feel about aging is also related to the fact that our particular society does not seem to value its older citizens as much as I believe we should. In much of today's popular culture, it seems that a stronger spirit and wiser mind are often not held in as high esteem or celebrated as much as the strong and young body. It seems to me that many Asian cultures have it right about respecting their elders as national treasures. These elders are at the pinnacle of their enlightenment and wisdom and have much to teach us. It behooves us all to appreciate and absorb everything we can from those who are older and wiser than we are while they are still present to share the accumulated gems of their lifetime. Now, if only I can convince my children and grandchildren of that!

Marking Time

HOLLY DEUEL GILSTER

"Old age ain't no place for sissies."
BETTE DAVIS

There was an old lady who swallowed a fly.
I don't know why she swallowed that fly.
Perhaps she'll die!

WE ALL KNOW "The Old Lady Who Swallowed a Fly," but when we sang about her as children, we never thought about who she actually was. And why did songs like that always have to be about the old? Does aging make one feeble? Have the elderly lost their ability to reason and therefore find themselves eating a variety of creatures? Or is it just silly nonsense with no meaning at all?

For years, I never believed it when people would say, "I looked in the mirror and suddenly saw an old person." Then I woke up one day, looked in the mirror and saw an old person. It was Wednesday, December 7, 2016. I remember the exact day. I looked at my swollen eyes and thought, "I must have pink eye." No, that wasn't it. "I must have a sinus infection." That wasn't it, either. "I must have allergies because my eyes are now red and weeping." Maybe.

Whatever the reason, I now have the face of a woman who has fought gravity for sixty years. And I don't like it!

I like to say that gravity sucks. It's supposed to be funny.

I look at my two flabby breasts that have nursed four children and then at young women with perky breasts, and I think, "Are those implants?" I can't remember a time when my breasts defied gravity. My ass is no longer round and bouncy when I walk to lure young men into the propagation of the species. No, it sits flat, tucked against my upper thighs. Not a bother to anybody, not an eyesore and not an attraction.

So if my body is no longer needed to continue the species, then my corporeal self is simply a vehicle for the spirit inside me that is continuing to evolve. When I look in the mirror, I see the body of a sixty-year-old. Yet I feel that my spirit is still in her thirties. It lends credence to the idea of reincarnation.

I posit that my spirit does not age. And by that I am not referring to my own maturity. If Spirit is ageless, then Spirit is not defined by the husk of a physical body and can therefore transcend the loss of that corpse. If that's the case why did I not feel my thirty-year-old spirit back when I was a six-year-old first-grader? Because, my six-year-old brain had not yet developed into my fully adult brain.

We know from current research that the adult brain does not kick in until our late twenties. Ironic isn't it? We call eighteen-year-olds adults, yet we deny them certain privileges, and rightly so. We call twenty-one-year-olds adults, yet these young people are incapable of making the kinds of thoughtful decisions that they will make when they have finally reached their maturity.

In the days before penicillin and advanced medicine, thirty was middle age and sixty-year-olds were nearing the end of their lifecycle. It's different today. Here I stand on the cusp of my sixtieth birthday and I realize that it's possible I might live another thirty years. Oy vey! An entire lifetime! What the hell do I do with it? I'm not driven to have children. I've done that. I'm not driven to stake out my place in my career field. I've done that. I've seen most of the world, although there are always new places to visit. So how do I make meaning out of the rest of it? I don't know yet.

Sometimes, I find the chasm of my extended lifespan overwhelming. When my children left home, it was the most devastating period of my life. I had raised them to be independent free-thinkers capable of supporting themselves. Then they went and proved me right! So now what do I do? I'm teaching in the career that I've always wanted. Now that career is coming to a close, and I've never wanted anything else. So again I say, "Now, what do I do?"

I know how to join clubs to keep myself busy. But being busy is not the same thing as having a purpose. I don't yet know how to have a purpose for the next thirty years of my life. It has occurred to me that I can just wait around for the odd moments my children need me, but that is not enough to sustain my sense of self. Certainly, that old woman who swallowed a fly has nothing useful to offer me.

So here I am about to turn sixty and I am not at all at ease with it. I pray for guidance from the God of my choosing but for now, I'm just marking time.

Sixty-Five Years Young!

KARLA "ROSIE" HARPER

*"As we grow old,
the beauty steals inward."*

RALPH WALDO EMERSON

GRAY IS MY LEAST favorite color. You won't find it in my hair, unless I'm due for a dye job. It's not in my closets or drawers, unless I bought a package of panties that had one gray among five others that were yellow and turquoise. It's definitely not in the color scheme of my home's decor. My car is bright yellow, my hair golden blonde. My garden is highlighted with yellow sunflowers, red and purple sages, pink geraniums and orange lilies. People call me sunshine. When I'm really old, I will continue to wear bright colors, not just purple.

At the chronological age of sixty-five, I am retired from my profession as a public school teacher. Now, I get to teach my grandchildren as we explore the world around us. I help lift the spirits of those older than myself by singing and dancing for folks in nursing homes. I get to eat lunch in restaurants with groups of girl-friends several times a month. I giggle and engage in lively conversations with the gals in my book club. My body and mind get plenty of exercise, as I am regularly learning new songs and dances, skiing, biking, swimming, romping with the little ones and traveling. I'm finally happily married after three failed attempts. Life is better than ever.

Sagging skin and drooping jowls make me

unhappy, though. I like looking pretty. When I'm all dolled up for a dance in a darling red dress and have my face made up with pretty colors, I can still turn heads. When I look at myself through the lens of FaceTime on my computer, however, I look like an old hag. Soft lighting and nearsightedness are my new best friends.

Youthful appearances rely on more than the elasticity of one's skin, however. Energy is also important. By the time I was in my fifties, I found I was losing my health and vitality. My body was acting as if everything in the world was a threat. I had irritable bowel syndrome, as my digestive system had become allergic to just about everything I was consuming. There were times my guts were so severely cramped that it took heavy drugs to settle them down. I was having frightening panic/anxiety attacks on a regular basis. I could barely stay awake for my afternoon classes at school. I couldn't stand heat, cold, high altitudes, wind, travel, the least little stressor. Although my job was difficult, it wasn't my job that was to blame.

Doctors and therapists, even naturopaths and acupuncturists, were unsuccessful in restoring my health. I needed someone who could uncover the real, deep cause of my troubles. I needed help finding my way back to being the free-spirited, cheerful, peppy gal that I was when I was young.

Quantum healing was what I needed. The

healer I found when I was fifty-nine turned out to be the one I'd been looking for all my life. She determined that my body had come to associate foods and environmental stressors with emotional traumas I'd experienced during the course of my life. She helped my body to disconnect the associations it had made. My body had also hung onto and stored a wide variety of toxic chemicals and heavy metals over the years. There were too many for it to deal with as time marched on. No wonder my body was unhealthy. How can organs and systems possibly work well when they are clogged up with gunk? Instead of being a well oiled machine, my body was a toxic waste dump.

Antibiotics had also played a role. They had upset the balance of my beneficial micro-organisms. Immune systems, digestion and metabolic processes all depend on these. I had to stop using all antibacterial products to give my body a chance to reestablish those little critters.

Psychologically, I was stopped up, too. Over and over in my life, people had been upset by my vivaciousness, my unfettered belly laugh, my thoughts and ideas that were outside of their box. They had been jealous of my talents and abilities, my cute little figure, my happiness and successes. They did and said things that shut me down. I ended up feeling guilty and ashamed of myself. Narcissists had me convinced I was a dysfunctional person, when all along they were the ones who were being difficult, not me.

Working with that gifted healer has brought my vitality back to the level of a thirty-year-old, so I'm telling my body every day that it can do anything it puts its mind to. If my vitality can be restored, perhaps my skin can, too. Perhaps my subcutaneous layer of fat can be rebuilt. It would be nice if my hands didn't look like a mass of just skin and bones, with big blue veins that pop up off the surface. It would be awesome if my gums would grow back so food doesn't get stuck in the spaces between my teeth. I'd save a few trees if I didn't need to use so many toothpicks.

Because of all the work I've done to free up my body, mind and spirit, I am *me at last*. After all these years, I am not only *still* me. I am *myself*, feeling more and more rejuvenated with each passing year.

The package I am in may not be as pretty as it was when I was thirty, but it bears many gifts I expect that it will keep on giving for many years to come.

Aging into Orphanhood

Maureen Polikoff

"The great secret that all old people share is that you really haven't changed in seventy or eighty years. Your body changes, but you don't change at all. And that, of course, causes great confusion."

Doris Lessing

THE DICTIONARY DEFINITION of "orphan" is direct and straightforward: "Someone whose parents are dead." Like defining one's child as "a person I gave birth to" or one's husband as "someone I married," the literal definition doesn't begin to uncover the complexities of how it feels to *be* an orphan. My parents were the first to define who I am, and I spent a good part of my life living up to, rejecting, exceeding or rebelling against those definitions.

My father died many years ago, my mother at the end of 2015, shortly before my sixtieth birthday. While I grieved the loss of my father and remember him with bittersweet sadness, my mother's death was a whole different ballgame. I felt as if the universe from which I came had shifted, and along with it, me. The depth of my loss remains impossible to describe. Part of it is my closer relationship with her, but beyond that is my own aging issues rising to the surface. At the youngish age of sixty, I had suddenly become the "elder generation." I wasn't ready for it, and I feel like an imposter at it most of the time. Aren't I still that young woman who believed that no matter how many years passed, I could still call Mom for comfort and advice when I got sick, hurt or upset? Couldn't I still share with her my joyful moments, dreams and accomplishments?

My anchor has become untethered, and I am now sailing freely through what feels at times like some pretty unknown and dangerous waters. I'm not ready to be the matriarch of anything, thank you very much. Ready or not, my definition of self and my role in my family is changing. I no longer have to think (or worry) about how my decisions will affect my parents. Both liberating and daunting, as I have used that boundary as a guide throughout my life.

My brother, with whom I have always been extremely close, went with me through the gut-wrenching task of dismantling my mother's life. While this strengthened an already unbreakable bond, it was heartbreaking for both of us to connect on that level, so I now find myself distancing myself from and avoiding him at times. My sister, who has many challenges in her life, was taken care of and enabled by my mother, often to my complete dismay. I find myself being far less judgmental of her, and feeling more kindness and empathy toward her. My husband, who has walked this difficult path with me every step of the way, has increasingly become my safe place to land, my assurance that I am not alone. The rest of my family is mainly becoming more splintered and fragmented, sadly. I am becoming the common denominator in that they can all "talk to me" (any surprise that I became a therapist?). Is it okay that that baton now appears to have been passed from my mother to me?

I feel older, somehow. I have hopefully channeled some of the wisdom of aging from my mother and I have a responsibility to honor that wisdom. I think about what she would have thought or said and have many conversations with her in my head. I worry more about my health. I think about money, pensions, retirement. I try not to get depressed about the fact that no matter how much I exercise I will never look like that twenty-five-year-old, or forty-year-old, or even fifty-year-old (damn!). I try to remember my mother's words: "This, too, shall pass." Or what she would say about living through difficult times, "It sure beats the alternative."

On the other hand, aging has been a liberating and empowering experience. I noticed it first in my fifties. I'm not as inclined to give a shit about what other people think of me, expect of me or want from me. I'm not as easily manipulated. Now that I am beyond the ripe old age of sixty (apparently that is when you graduate from being middle-aged to aging), I am more confident in my professional expertise and accomplishments. I'm not as afraid. I recognize my own solid instincts and good judgment. When I get pissed off at the world, it's not because of what it is not giving me, but because of what it is taking from all of us. I realize that no one can be on a guilt trip unless they buy a ticket. I know the importance of kindness and love above all else.

Perhaps there is a connection between all of this and becoming an orphan, not having a parent to fall back on. Or to blame. It's time to truly be a grown-up. To take what was learned either willingly or through fighting it, kicking and screaming...and use it.

Thanks, Mom.

The Minefield of Aging

Aaron Gordon

"Wisdom comes with winters."

Oscar Wilde

FROM MY VANTAGE POINT NOW at ninety years of age, I can see that the aging process, depending on how long one lives, goes through various stages. When I turned sixty-five and retired from teaching, that sort of was a marker for me that, yeah, I'm moving up the age ladder. But it really didn't impact me in any significant way. It didn't alter my life pattern. I was just giving up my work and moving into another phase of life in which I thought, well, retirement can offer a lot of different options, which it did.

At that age (sixty-five) I remember going to a movie and asking the young woman in the box office for a senior ticket and saying, "even though you might not think I'm a senior." I didn't really view myself as a senior, but I realized I was entitled to that benefit. That hung in with me for awhile.

Basically in my sixties and into early seventies, very little changed about how I felt about myself. I was aware I was getting older but it didn't represent a profound change in my thinking other than wondering what I was going to do with my freedom.

As you get older, you do realize there will be an end, but you don't know when that will come. I had already been through a pre-aging set of occurrences in which I underwent major bypass surgery at age fifty. Suddenly, there was a "mortality reality" to what I was undergoing. Thirty years later, when I was close to eighty, I had a second bypass operation: yet another confrontation with the fact that I was dealing with a life that could suddenly be brought to an end.

During that interim between bypass surgeries, my wife was diagnosed with breast cancer and had surgery. That was a serious moment in time when I worried about losing her. I realized we were entering a phase of life in which things were beginning to happen. It forced me to pause and think about that reality. But as it happened, I came through fine and so did my wife. Life moved on.

As I think about the aging process, the thing that most preoccupies my thoughts is what's in store for me; not in terms of life and death, but what's it going to be like to be older. In my sixties, we had already lost a few friends to cancer and heart disease, so those are moments when you pause and realize, yes, that's part of life — giving it up. On the other hand, that never became something I focused on, so throughout my seventies I maintained pretty decent health and physical activity.

It was in my mid-seventies that I began to sense there were things I couldn't do as easily as I did before, and that we had to give up certain activities like cross-country skiing; it became too hard to handle that wonderful experience we had once shared. As I moved into later years, I remember telling my wife, "I think you need to give up bicycle riding; you're not as steady as you once were." Then, when I was eighty-two and we moved to Albuquerque, I took out my bike (which I had been riding for many, many years), and by golly, I went out for a ride and said, "I think this is it. It's too hard. Albuquerque is not the flatlands of Illinois."

Over the course of time, talking with friends during my seventies and early eighties, we began to discuss aging, confronting a life pattern that felt like walking through a mine-field. You've got to be careful. Things were beginning to happen (not to me personally, but to contemporaries). People were beginning to feel that with aging comes limits. And that was bothersome. And to this day, that remains my principle concern — the limits. I remember, ten years ago, when I was eighty, my wife and I were in Barcelona, Spain and had rented an apartment for two weeks. We were on our own and at the conclusion of that two-week tour, it became obvious that this probably would be our last overseas trip. It was just getting too hard getting into subways and managing steps, and the sheer amount of walking that we had so enjoyed in the past we could no longer do.

For me, the aging process has been a gradual awareness of having to give up certain things that were enjoyable and wondering what's next down the line. The primary issue for me is not the issue of death. I think about it (although I don't like to think about it). And sometimes I can even joke about it. But my principle sense now, at ninety — and for the last few years with my wife having a recurrence of cancer — is that, yes, death is on my mind. But more than that is what happens to us as we continue to age, and to age beyond the point that we ever thought we would live. You see, at age fifty, when I was diagnosed with heart disease and had a triple bypass, which at that time was a relatively unknown procedure, I remember taking my first stress test after the surgery. I got on the treadmill and I was fine. The cardiologist and I celebrated that moment and we sat down to talk about the future. It was clear from his point of view that I had every reason to believe I would live a normal life, providing I changed a few life patterns. I turned to him and said, "Doc, if you can get me into my early to mid-seventies, I'll be happy with that." When we decided to do a second bypass when I was eighty, I asked him, "What can I count on now?" He said "We'll see."

So, am I concerned about the aging process at this point? You bet I am. I'm in a facility where I see exactly what age has offered up to my fellow residents, and it's not a pretty picture. And I often wonder and worry about what lies ahead for me. I don't want to wind up in a wheelchair being pushed around by a caregiver. That just doesn't feel right. I've been healthy and physically very active in spite of my medical history. So that's my primary worry, along with worries about my partner. I often think about what life will be like if she passes before me. And I worry what would happen to her if I pass before her. And I think those are the major worries when one reaches my stage in life.

What gives me a boost when I begin to feel overwhelmed with what may happen in the future and on those days when I really feel my age is recognizing there are people living in this retirement community who have suffered not only from age, but from serious health problems like strokes. Some of these residents are an inspiration to me because, despite the terrible limits that have been imposed on them, and they're significantly younger than I am, they're working hard at overcoming their disability to the extent they can. I see them in the gym working to regain some ability to walk or to use a hand that is unable to grasp a fork or a knife or even hold a cane. So that's kind of an up-side and I realize that, despite what lies ahead, I like to think I have some degree of inner strength to cope if something like that were to happen to me.

About five years ago, as I became increasingly aware of a gradual loss of visual acuity, we moved into a retirement community because I had to give up driving. At that point, I fully realized that aging involves walking through a minefield and boy, I stepped on a live one.

That was a blow, you might say, a real confrontation with not just age, but with what comes with age. Because the vision problem, macular degeneration, is age-related. And with that, I began to lose the ability to read and ultimately the ability to write. I'm at that point where I can do neither. This loss of vision has also presented difficulties with respect to where I live. I'm in a large social setting in which I know people but cannot recognize them in the dining room. And that always leaves me feeling less than whole.

One can say the minefield that is aging became a reality at that point. Earlier, I mentioned that I've been inspired by some of the fellow residents who are confronting major disabling issues and struggle to sustain themselves with meaningful activities. In being aware of them, I've also at times, reflected on my own situation and tried hard to assert a sense of how I can cope with my problem and overcome the disabling affects of it. To that end, I've become a listener to audiobooks. At first it was hard to give up the idea of holding a book in my hands and reading, as well as writing. Needless to say, both of these activities were basic to my whole life because I was a college professor for some thirty-three years. At any rate, I've made the transition and, in the past couple of years, I've managed to listen to some of the great classics. I've decided that I don't need to keep up-to-date wth current fiction. I need to go back and listen to the great classics I never had the opportunity to spend time with. That has been a very satisfying activity for me. Also, I've discovered that the computer, on which I had been able to do some writing before but can no longer really do, offered me an opportunity to listen to the phenomenon of podcasts. And I discovered YouTube. Up close, I can see fine. I continue to watch TV, but can only do that with my face almost pressed against the screen.

It's been a real journey. The key is just having the strength and willpower to cope with the realities of aging, which clearly indicate that there are going to be limits, there are going to be areas of independence that you have to give up. It's nice having someone do the cooking for us. I've made the adjustment to using the transportation our retirement facility provides to get to appointments.

I remain intellectually active. I still follow the daily events occurring in our world, some of which are difficult to follow but nonetheless are part of the life setting. And that's the part of me that I hope continues to provide vitality as I move into these very late years, which, who knows, could end tomorrow, a year from now, two years from now. There's no way of knowing. All I can do is carry on as best I can.

As he notes in his essay, Aaron Gordon is no longer able to see clearly enough to either read or write. He dictated this essay to me. – Karen Helene Walker

All in the Family

MARY CLARK

"And yet the wiser mind
Mourns less for what
age takes away
Than what it leaves behind."

WILLIAM WORDSWORTH

FOR YEARS I THOUGHT family traits had played their hand only in my early development: brown hair from the Scotch-Irish relatives, musical talent from a maternal grandmother, Uncle Rusty's sense of humor. An early appearance of migraine headaches was traced to my great-aunt. Adeptness at math came from Mom's side of the family. As my personality developed, I assumed I was on my own and gene connections were done.

I was wrong. As I matured, I came to realize that latent genes had been waiting patiently beneath the surface, ready to reveal themselves only in later years.

My Mother's Hands

I have my mother's hands. This was a late-in-life discovery. Not much of Mom's DNA ever reflected in my outer looks, apart from my height...or lack of it. Dad's genes dominated: fair skin, freckles, thin lips. But I had always loved my mother's hands with their beautiful proportions and strong, protruding veins. I would notice them as she stroked her favorite dog in her lap or licked her fingers from making one more cake, or when she drove me home from the airport. As she aged, capillary-sized wrinkles may have filled the spaces between knuckles, but her wedding band and mother's rings continued to fit nicely. Despite arthritis in other parts of her body, her hands never gnarled.

After Mom died, I inherited her mother's engagement and wedding rings and began to wear them on my right hand as she had done. One day, I looked at my hands and realized they were hers: nicely proportioned, strong protruding veins, capillary-sized wrinkles, family rings. I'd had to age into them, to catch up in years, to fill in with wrinkles, before I could know whose hands I really had. It was a lovely surprise and now keeps Mom close while lessening the pain of aging skin.

The "Ideas Gene"

I've long been an idea person, an organized woman, one who prefers being in charge. It's easy for me to see what needs to be done and how to do it. Over the years, these mental gymnastics have included putting meals together, arranging furniture, starting a girls' soccer league, raising money and planning trips, all in addition to practicing law and having children.

Outside the family, the community loved my boundless energy. Inside the family, it often exhausted my husband, who felt pressured by my constant bursts of ideas. It became a negative in our relationship as I wondered what I could do to slow down the onslaught. Two discoveries helped both of us accept this trait of mine.

The first involved my maternal grandmother, Irene, who died when my mother was five. Not surprisingly, Mom remembered little about her. Later, as a young mother, I approached a great-aunt and asked for a description of my grandmother. In the opening line of her letter, Aunt Luella wrote, "Irene was the idea person. She organized the games at parties and made things happen." This description could easily have been of my mother, or of me. Grateful and relieved, I showed my husband the letter, pointing out that I couldn't help myself. The "ideas gene" had been passed down to me.

The second discovery confirmed that the "ideas gene" was still a dominant trait in my family's maternal line. It was after our daughter Ellen became a mother that she and I started finishing each other's sentences. Each of us knew when the other would be upset about a political statement or when a shortsighted law passed. Our unorthodox religious beliefs lined up. Public education was important to us both. But, mainly, our identical ideas often arrived and were spoken simultaneously. Neither of us could help it. They just showed up without asking permission.

This new facet of our relationship had important consequences for our family. First,

I was now more comfortable with my idea side without feeling as though I had to make apologies for it. Clearly, the "ideas gene" was as much a part of my daughter's DNA and mine as it had been for my mother and grandmother. This ability was not to be ignored.

My husband was also affected after watching his beloved daughter take after his wife: community leader, active social life, involved with her children and outspoken on politics. He and I had to mature enough to accept what I was and to work together on how to use that tendency of mine judiciously, adjusting it according to our respective energy levels.

I never expected my grandmother and daughter to give me permission to be me but they did. A gene is not to be denied.

The DNA of Health

As the only girl in a family of five children, I never looked for shared traits with my brothers as we grew up, even as we all had allergies and asthma. I did girl stuff and they did boy stuff, and nothing else mattered.

After leaving home, we scattered across three states and thousands of miles. We try to gather every other year but often one or more can't come. It may be several years between visits, even though we occasionally chat by phone or share information through emails. Only in more recent years, though, has our health been a subject of those get-togethers, chats and emails.

My older brother was the first to announce he had high blood pressure. Later, the middle brother and I had daily headaches until our doctors informed us that we, too, had high blood pressure. The fourth brother wrote to warn about having high blood pressure without realizing three of us were already being treated for it. Then, my youngest brother had a stroke.

Since then, I've watched three of my brothers' hair disappear, thanks to Mom's baldness gene. I search for words as my mother often did. When recently looking through old photos of my paternal grandmother in her sixties, I realized that I favor her even more now than I did as a young woman.

The ancestor's connections continue, bringing home to me even more eloquently the genetic component of my health and aging.

Sometimes, I fret over how all that will play out as I enter the world of the elderly. My mother had aphasia and loss of memory, small strokes and died of cancer. But, then, my grandmother lived to be a hundred and was sharp to the end. Which aging genes landed in my DNA? Which side of the family will dominate as I continue to age?

In the old days, we had to grow old for those and other genetic secrets to reveal themselves. Today, thanks to genetic testing, some of those secrets are no longer secret. I'm grateful that I can be warned about the potentially dangerous medical conditions that I might be carrying in my DNA. As for any remaining revelations resulting from the genes that are all in my family, I would still rather be surprised.

An Ode on Being Eighty-Two

FRAN FISCHER

*"Ah! Si je n'avais que
quatre-vingts ans. /
Oh, would that I were but
eighty years old."*

BERNARD LE BOVIER DE FONTENELLE

My legs are sore. I need a cane.
My body has gone quite insane.
My breasts were perky as a song.
My bra size now is 40-Long.

I cannot hear. I cannot see.
I have to pee. Oh, woe is me!
My body's fat. My skin is thin.
I do not like the shape I'm in.

I cough — I cough until I choke.
I'm going out to have a smoke.
My bones are brittle, I fear my fate.
I'm liable to disintegrate.

My memory now seems to have gone.
Who is that standing on my lawn?
It's my husband Bud — or is his name Paul?
I thought he died — I can't recall.

The thermometer says it's sixty-three.
I don't know why it lies to me.
I can't stop sweating–watch me pour.
My body says it's 104.

My joints creak and pop so bad
I'm like a steel drum from Trinidad.
Leg cramps woke me again last night.
Why is my skin so loose and my muscles tight?

My health is iffy. I may not thrive.
But life is good — and I'm still alive!
And I hope I'll be around to see
What I'm like at eighty-three!

Roses in November

WENDY BROWN

"*It is better to be seventy years young than forty years old.*"

OLIVER WENDELL HOLMES

LATE LAST NOVEMBER I walked out of my home in Albuquerque and noticed a cluster of luscious red roses blooming on the bush that greets visitors approaching our door. Roses in November! In New Mexico this is a most unexpected gift. Frosts typically begin in September, and by November have occurred frequently enough to discourage even the most enthusiastic plants from venturing to bloom.

Channeling my mother — "waste nothing, create beauty and grace wherever possible!" — I clipped the flowers and placed them in an elegant black vase to backdrop their brilliant color. My husband and I enjoyed them for a long time at the dining room table and as winter approached, those fragrant petals evoked thoughts and memories about my own life.

Now let me just say, I don't feel that I'm in the November of my life. Retired from my career, yes. Well past childbearing age or turning a lot of heads when I walk down the street, yes. But blessed with the genes of a long-lived family, abundant vitality and good health to date, I would say I'm more like early August. What does that mean?

For me, August is a time for harvest of summer's bounty. It is also a time for new beginnings (an artifact from decades of school attendance) and a time to prepare for the enforced quietude of winter. The bounty of this time of my life is the fruits of the work I've done till now. Many years of formal schooling led to a rich career in wildlife biology: adventures, travel, being out there and often right up front in the heart of work that I loved — trying to restore endangered species such as wolves and whooping cranes amid the tumultuous politics and emotions attached to these creatures. This work both consumed and molded me.

But all along the schooling and work of life shaped me, as it does us all. People: lovers, friends, family, mentors, rivals, even the homeless man on the street outside my office. Relationships shaped me. Relationships taught me that dancing in the world with others, however imperfectly, is far more satisfying in the end than the best solo performance. Grief schooled me. The death of my sister from alcoholism at forty-three was my first real lesson in mortality, and humility. I couldn't save her; that was her job, and my well-intentioned attempts to do so were a form of arrogance. Hardship trained me: losing my first job due to a sharp right turn in federal administration. Divorce... childlessness: These things taught me not to count on anything worthwhile being easy, but I learned that I could free fall for a long time and land on my feet. Dogs, my most consistent companions since childhood, have taught me more about being in the present moment than have all those books on mindfulness I've read. But, yes, books: Reading has been one of the greatest gifts of my life. Authors far too numerous to name have offered their stories — words, insights, wisdom, joys and sorrows expressed in ways that have permeated my soul.

Finally, my Elders, those wise people who offered what was needed in ways I could receive: love, patience, endurance and examples of lives well-lived. They have all passed on now, and I miss them. I do channel them, not as often nor as perfectly as I would like. But they are the source of my grounding on this earth.

So, that's a taste of my harvest — some of the best of my life's garden to this point. And while I hope to keep gardening for a long while yet, the focus of my life at this stage is that new beginning that will use my harvest for the greatest good...and for the preparation of my coming winter's quietude.

Like most folks, my retirement from a career was an enormous leap into the unknown. After two years and lots of exploration, I'm still finding my way. But I'm honing my navigation skills as I go, and the path I'm following is that of yoga.

I have practiced asana (the physical postures of yoga) for over twenty years, and like most Westerners, I thought yoga was the asana. As a very physical person, I knew that asana practice strengthened and challenged me, felt good and helped me to become calmer, more grounded. But along the way, I began to realize that yoga was so much more than that.

In the formal study of yoga, asana is only one limb of the eight-limbed path. The others involve aspects of living discipline such as moral restraints and observances of being in the world, mindful breathing, self-study, concentration, meditation and uniting with a higher power. Some form of these practices can be found in any religion or sacred text... and in thousands of self-help books.

I know that yoga is not the only path, but it's an ancient path that has persisted for thousands of years, and it speaks to me in ways that others have not.

I look forward to continuing my practice of all the limbs of yoga for the rest of my life. As I am about to complete two hundred hours of teacher training, I'll continue to study. But I'll also seek ways to offer what I've learned to others. It's fine that I don't know exactly what that looks like right now. It might be teaching to dancers, or it might be offering yoga to paraplegics. The idea of teaching to prison inmates has called to me. Perhaps it won't involve regular teaching at all.

One of the blessings of this age is that I am so much more at peace with uncertainty. I don't have to prove anything, and thank God I don't have to earn a living based on my current exploration.

Another great gift is that I have made the acquaintance of mortality. I try not to look at impermanence as a hard boundary, but rather as a supple frame for living each moment — focusing on those things that nourish me and others. Right now, it's the deep study of yoga. But it's also taking the time to love the life I have today: a devoted husband, a community of friends that love to dance, the children and grandchildren of my sister, my dogs, the birds that grace our backyard, the hiking I can still do, the sunrise every morning.

I'll keep on gardening as long as I can, and perhaps I'll have those roses in November, whenever it arrives.

Am I Now "Officially" Old?

KAREN NORSTAD

"None are so old as those who have outlived enthusiasm."

ANONYMOUS

YESTERDAY, I TURNED SEVENTY-FOUR. I never expected to live this long, given the poor longevity of women on my mother's side. However, here I am and I'm glad to still be here. Over the past week, I have been wondering if I am now officially an Old Person. I'm definitely not "middle-aged," since nobody yet lives to be one hundred and forty-eight. I am pretty healthy, thanks to my blood pressure and cholesterol meds and, despite an extra twenty pounds, I am still able to walk around, climb stairs and do everything I need to do, including assembling IKEA furniture. So, does it even make any difference if I'm now an Old Person?

The reason this came up is that I seem to have reached a tipping point, where I can now really see the changes that have slowly accumulated over the past ten years. For example, the whole daily body-upkeep routine is much more labor intensive. The shower: being careful not to slip while washing feet (phone within reach, of course); always putting lotion on after shower — one that smells good to ward off any possible Old Lady smell (I've devoted considerable online research to the origins and prevention of Old Man smell. The Japanese excel at this); immediate moisturizer on face. Then underwear, always including leakage protection at the lowest level that works (not ready for Attends yet!), clothes (avoid shirts that show flappy arms) and shoes. Shoes were never a problem before, but since wearing a pair of ill-fitting ones too often, I now have a constantly sore big toe.

At this point, I need to take a break before teeth-cleaning and makeup.

Brushing teeth is a ten-minute process driven by periodontal edicts. Missing teeth in the back, luckily not visible, are a testimony to decades of war against periodontal disease.

Next is the often depressing survey of the day's face. Did I sleep wrong and make lines that won't go away until the evening? Did I end up with bags under one or both eyes today? Is it time to shave the peach fuzz off my face again? It's a dead giveaway for an aging woman and starts around middle age. I never noticed it until I overheard a conversation among men at work one day where a woman was described as having a lot of "that peach fuzz on her face that older women get." I went home that night and shaved my face. A personal groomer/shaver is best, not a razor. And don't forget to check for any visible nose hairs!

Putting on makeup: Foundation, concealer, try to be sure the blush doesn't just high-light the eye-bags but also gives your face the intended rosy glow. Eye makeup and the art of creating eyelids where there weren't any. Some days are better than others, when I actually do have visible eyelids. Then eyeliner — does it really help? It looks great on some women, but is it looking good on me? Eyebrows — fill in the thinning parts with pencil but make it look "natural." Curl eyelashes — mascara, too. I notice that my eyelashes are turning gray. But the worst is lipstick. How to keep it from feathering into the lines now radiating from my lips. Which color is better? Does a lipliner help?

Then there's hair. Poor hair, years of coloring, blowdrying and other abuse. Where's that hairdo that some women have that always looks phenomenal whatever their decade and right into old age? I'm still looking. Too-short hair and the thinness shows. The main thing is to be sure there are no places on my head where, when combed, there are obvious thin spots. My hair wants to part in weird places, and they look like bald spots. So, it's teasing and spraying...more time than I want to spend on this. All so that a person behind me in line at the grocery store won't think I have a bald spot. Did an especially bad hair-color job last time and a chunk of silver gray is showing. I wonder how I would look with silver hair, but am not ready to find out. To me, gray hair equals invisibility. Total and complete. I'm already fifty percent invisible.

According to average-life-expectancy charts for the United States, I can expect to live at least five more years. Now *that* is something to think about. Relative to the question I ask in the title, that pretty much puts me in the one-foot-in-the-grave-and-the-other-on-a-banana-peel category. I'm inclined to think/hope it's realistic to project ten more years. Still, not much.

The most remarkable part of growing old, I think, is how fast it happens. It seems like no time at all. Years fly by, faster the older you get. The familiar markers come and go: seasons, holidays, birthdays. Also, the realization of how impossible it was to really imagine yourself as an old person when you were younger. It seemed so very far away, even in middle age. Perhaps some other cultures live with a heightened sense of impending mortality, but I think it's just not in our human makeup to think that way, unless we live in a war zone or have another good reason to think death is imminent.

Anyway, now that I'm here, I find that I am expected to have formed a cohesive philosophy or general set of comforting beliefs about my eventual demise. The truth is, I have absolutely no idea what will happen when I die. It seems equally likely that I will simply cease to exist, that we are all living in some cosmic interactive video game and I'll pop out of my avatar and continue to live on another plane in some highly advanced civilization or that we really do reincarnate into new lives. Heaven and hell are not on my radar, but I do allow for the possibility of ghosts and also for other planes of reality coexisting with this one.

As for reflecting on one's life, it can be painful. Hopefully, time and experience have offered a more objective perspective on some of the main stumbling blocks, character traits and personal challenges we've coped with over a lifetime. Some have been tempered by a better perspective — forgiveness of ourselves and others, for example. Some are still actively with us. Relative to the death experience, I read a thought-provoking article the other day in *The New York Times* about Hospice by the Bay, a zen hospice in San Francisco. Dr. B. J. Miller, its former director, noted our "need for death to be a hypertranscendent experience" and stated that "most people aren't having these transformative deathbed moments. If you hold that out as a goal, they're just going to feel like they're failing." That was somehow comforting. One less expectation to live up to.

Truth is, I spend very little time thinking about death. I'm way too busy doing laundry, cooking, paying bills and keeping up with friends and family. I enjoy my little garden of flowering plants and the beauty of the world, playing my piano, keeping up with politics, reading and just enjoying being alive now and for as long as I am still here.

Hallelujah and pass the birthday cake! I'm an Old Person!

Just Another Journey

Patricia Stoltey

*"To grow old is to pass
from passion to compassion."*

Albert Camus

AT SEVENTY-FOUR I have physical challenges that change my plans almost daily. If my arthritic back or joints hurt, I can't sit at the computer or walk the dog very long. If my fibromyalgia acts up, I just want to take a long nap. I accept all that. Bette Davis is credited with the quote, "Old age ain't no place for sissies." She was right.

But old age is a relative thing. My mother was ninety-seven in May 2016. She has osteo- and rheumatoid arthritis. At the end of October 2012, she had a tiny stroke and was put on hospice. She didn't care for that much, so she willed herself to get better and graduated in just a few weeks. An old hip replacement dislocated several times after she had a fall and twisted out of its socket. My brother was very ill at the time, so I went to Illinois (from Colorado where I live) and moved Mom from her apartment to assisted living for better supervision. She did well for a time, but in February 2015 she fell in the bathroom and fractured her good hip.

We used to consider a hip fracture the end of the road for the elderly. My mom wasn't having any of that! Even with the limitations put on her by the orthopedic surgeon that restricted her mobility and pretty much put her in a wheel-chair, Mom kept moving as much as she could.

A motorized wheelchair kept her independent so she could still go from room to room and to the dining room or the activities area on her own.

I was out of action a lot in 2015, first with a broken foot and later with a total knee replacement. And sadly, my brother's health continued to deteriorate, so he could no longer visit our mother. He passed away the day after I got home from the hospital from knee surgery. That was tough on all of us, but especially Mom. She and my brother had been very close. But she stayed strong...despite a bad foot infection followed by a bout with pneumonia.

In addition to the condition of our own bodies as we age, and the length of time we or our parents will live, there's something else we cannot count on: convenient timing.

I couldn't deal with all those things from a distance through the winter. I wanted to get my mother moved so I could supervise her care better and visit her a couple times a week or more instead of twice a year. Her eyesight was dimming rapidly from her macular degeneration. Her hearing had deteriorated and her one hearing aid helped only a little. She was too isolated from family.

We finally got the move done in early September 2016. One of my daughters-in-law joined us in Illinois, helped with packing and organizing, then shared the driving with me to move Mom to a skilled nursing facility in my town in Colorado.

For a few moments, I could take a deep breath and relax.

But only for a few moments.

Mom's October Social Security direct deposit disappeared into the twilight zone.

The Social Security Administration does not recognize power of attorney as a valid representative. I am my mother's federal fiduciary for her Veterans Administration Aid and Attendance Allowance, but that does not translate to the Social Security system. Separate ballgame.

From solving the complex Social Security problem to simply registering Mom to vote, it has been one challenge after another. Every few days, I wonder how the elderly manage to wade through the bureaucratic swamp if they don't have a relative familiar with finances and applications and computers.

I wonder about my own well-being and my husband's as we get older. We have kids, but they don't live nearby. Maybe a little planning is in order? I have a talented friend whose husband must go into a memory care facility for his own safety and for my friend's physical and emotional well-being. It's a horrible dilemma. The husband's body held up but his mind did not. The other side of the coin is my mom. Her body has failed her in a multitude of ways, but her mind is very good for a ninety-seven-year-old.

It's all a jumble. Anyone who has dealt with an elderly parent or spouse with dementia or a debilitating condition or disease knows a version of this story. We can't prepare for every life complication, but a bit of prudent effort is wise. Like making sure we've done due diligence on assigning durable and health powers of attorney. Like clearing out and decluttering our homes ourselves instead of leaving it to others. Like making our aging and end-of-life wishes known to those who will look out for us.

In my younger years, I worried more about dying than aging. As a teen, I wondered if I would still be alive at the turn of the century when I'd be fifty-eight. As it turned out, I took my backpack that year and spent ten days solo in Norway to check out my roots, meet my mother's elderly cousins and travel. At sixty-five, my first novel was published. My mom was still playing golf when she was seventy, even after knee and hip replacements.

At any age, we are what our minds let us be and we do what our bodies allow. Mom said "no way" when she was put on hospice at ninety-three. She's done well for someone whose doctor had given up on her after a tiny stroke.

I can learn a lot from my mother, even after all these years. Now she's frail and wears out easily, but she paid attention to every bit of the 2016 election shenanigans, made her choice and voted. Even though she didn't watch each game of the Cubs march to win the World Series, she caught the news about the team and kept up on their wins and losses.

When I take her out for a ride or to my house for a visit, she spends a lot of time petting the dog and wishing our cat would finally warm up to her. And Mom never turns down a milk-shake on the drive back to her place.

That's the lesson.

We can find joy every moment of our lives, even during the hard times. If I can follow Mom's example as I grow older, taking pleasure in the things I can still do and letting those others things go, I'll be happy.

If I can continue to adapt to the new me, let myself evolve into this new Patricia the writer, as I've done at other ages with real-life jobs and with retirement, I'll be content.

If I always embrace life, its downs as well as its ups, I'll be grateful. My mother has done that with grace and enthusiasm.

Aging is just another journey, and I want to enjoy every moment of the trip.

On Dreams, Appetites and Possibilities

LD MASTERSON

"What helps with aging is serious cognition — thinking and understanding. You have to truly grasp that everybody ages. Everybody dies. There is no turning back the clock. So the question in life becomes: What are you going to do while you're here?"

GOLDIE HAWN

THERE'S A JOKE making the rounds about a woman who believes her house is haunted because every time she tries to look in the mirror, some old woman's face gets in the way.

I know the feeling.

The funny thing about getting old is how easy you forget it's happening. The gray hair is no big deal. Or the crows' feet, or the saggy double chin. When you look in the mirror a kind of filter kicks in that lets you check if your hair is combed and your clothes are straight without ever seeing those other things. Not long ago I was riding a shuttle bus and an older woman got on so I started to give her my seat. My husband stopped me and pointed out that she was probably younger than I am.

Oops. I forgot.

There are reminders. My knees are shot, so no more jogging. I huff and puff like a steam engine after one flight of stairs. My breakfast includes a pill for my heart, a pill for my stomach and a pill for my achy joints. Oh, I can still give something my all, I just reach all sooner than I used to.

There are some upsides. Sales people have a much harder time selling me something with a thirty-year warranty. If I forget something, I can blame my gray hair (senior moment). And there are some nice senior discounts floating around out there, if I think to ask for them.

What I find hard is the reality of diminishing possibilities.

When I was eighteen, anything was possible. A recruiter came to our school and I visualized myself in Navy white, sailing the seven seas. Or flying the friendly skies as a stewardess (long before they became flight attendants). I was an indifferent student back then so college wasn't part of my plan, but I was still going to have a good job and my own apartment. Maybe I'd find a roommate and we'd have parties and date cute, interesting guys. Or acting — I thought I'd be good at acting. Travel sounded fun. And I wanted to learn to ride — for real, not just sit on a horse. Of course, I'd fall in love, get married and have a whole bunch of kids. That was a given. Oh, and I wanted to be a writer. To write a book and see it on the shelf of a bookstore someday.

Lots of dreams and any one of them could come true.

Then I was in my mid-twenties. I was married and had two beautiful sons. My husband was active-duty Air Force, so I wasn't joining the Navy, and I'd moved directly from my parents' home to an apartment with my husband, so no bachelorette pad for me, either. But I wasn't unhappy; my life was full and busy and satisfying. I don't remember even thinking of the dreams I'd set aside. I could always go back to them...well, most of them.

By my mid-thirties, there was an odd sense of urgency about my dreams. I had to be the best mom ever. The college that didn't matter before mattered now. Once the boys were in school, I needed to find that dream job. Organizations I was part of were always giving awards to members for thirty, forty, even fifty years of service. Oh, yeah, I wanted one of those someday. I wrote a truly awful book and stuffed it in a drawer. One of my friends was having a wild, passionate affair. Well, maybe that wasn't my dream but...was I missing something? I think my thirties were less about dreams and more about questions. What was I missing out on?

Mid-forties. Empty nest. So many things I'd wanted to do as a mom but now it was too late. I guess this was my first "too late." The realization that the time for something had passed and I'd never get it back. As my interests changed, so did the things I was involved in. Joining new organizations now meant less chance of a longevity award later. I was still hanging on to other dreams. I'd managed two years of college before falling into a good job, but I was going to go back and get my four-year degree. I could still have that torrid affair. And there was another book, not quite as bad, tucked away in the drawer.

Fifties! Menopause. Grandchildren. A fresh start. Instead of feeling officially old, I took off on a whole new path. The grandkids were my chance to redo anything I thought I'd muffed with my own kids. I was going to be the best grandmother ever. I even started running, worked my way up to some pretty respectable times in 5k races and lost sixty pounds to go with it so the little ones wouldn't remember me as a fat old lady who couldn't do things with them. My job was going well and I enjoyed lots of activities. No time for an affair, but I'm sure I could have had one if I'd wanted. My third book found an agent, if not a publisher. This growing old thing was a piece of cake.

Then my mother died.

I was holding her hand and felt her life leave her. I helped the hospice nurse bathe her body and dress her in a fresh gown before the funeral home people arrived. I brushed her hair and kissed her goodbye. I reached for the faith of my childhood, long neglected...and it wasn't there.

For me, that was the beginning of being old. Mortality had showed its scary face. I started thinking of all the things I'd wanted to do with my life but hadn't. So many were no longer even a possibility. All those dreams wasted.

I started going to church, to rebuild my relationship with God and, thankfully, He was waiting for me. I was able to lean on Him a couple of years ago, when my dad went to be with Mom.

It's scary. My husband and I have moved up

to the top of the ladder. The next generation to go. I try not to dwell on it. Instead I focus on my family, my dreams, my possibilities.

I'm sixty-seven. My relationship with God is the strongest it's ever been. I'm still married to that same wonderful guy and I don't waste much time thinking about having an affair. I have a close, loving relationship with my sons and their wives. I've enjoyed every moment of watching my grandkids grow — the two oldest will leave the nest in the spring — and I hope to see them get married and maybe hold my great-grandchildren someday. I'm not in great physical shape, but I can do most of the things I want to do. I could still go back to school, or even learn to ride a horse (but I don't think I will). And I'm currently hunting for an agent for book number...oh, who's counting?

There are lots of dreams I'm never going to see happen. My possibilities are fewer. The scope of the menu is not as wide. But the restaurant is still open, and my appetite is just fine.

I feel wistful a little sad

Facing Forward

E.V. LEGTERS

*"To honor an old man
is showing respect to God."*

MUHAMMAD

ABRUPTLY, I BEGAN THINKING about age. Abruptly, the words "retirement" and "social security" and "Medicare" became part of my daily vocabulary. Abruptly, images of my eventual and inevitable doddering became constant.

My children, while fully grown, haven't yet determined their long-term agendas. There are no daughters-in-law in sight, no grandchildren. The house I love, bought after a divorce to give my sons a home base, is usually without them. The aftermath of funding cuts that recently eliminated my job reveals painfully real age discrimination. I understand the ramifications of a fixed income. My post-divorce "how to pay the bills" has become "is there anywhere pleasant to live within my means?" Where can I go that won't feel as though I've given up?

I turned sixty-five only last month, a point at which a doctor's appointment suddenly includes asking me whether I have fallen lately. I have not fallen lately. I can't recall falling at all. But I can say that my first novel was published earlier this year. That my second is due out next spring. I wrote all sorts of stories all the while I held all sorts of jobs — advertising and teaching and being a mom. I wrote all the while believing the day would come I'd write — and read and think and paint — full-time.

Instead of cobbling together part-time, some-times soul-sucking gigs to make ends meet, should I sell this house, however lovely...?

Okay, but to go where? How can I avoid self-pitying despair? Not in a rented room. Probably not as a life-long Northeast resident transplanted to the widely-acclaimed-to-be-affordable Deep South. Maybe my cobbled-together part-time jobs aren't so bad.

Then, during an ordinary lunch, an extraordinary idea.

"Did you know," my lunch companion asked, "that you can live in Portugal for half of what it costs here?"

I did not.

From the time I was twenty, I'd had a pre-monition-like sense that I'd live abroad for at least a few years. I envisioned the Lake District in England, or a town outside of Paris, or Florence. But choices in husbands and jobs kept this notion out of reach, and now sounded expensive.

Portugal? Is it true?

It's true.

And not only Portugal. Websites list all sorts of far-flung places that are more affordable than Connecticut. Malaysia and Ecuador. Belize. The south of France. Italy's Adriatic coast. Portugal.

Could I make this happen? Could I go through the difficult process of clearing my house of possessions — children's artwork, hundreds of books, family antiques, treasures collected from long-ago travels — to mobilize? Could a woman alone navigate visa regulations, foreign real-estate offices, foreign languages and, ultimately, solitude in a strange neighborhood?

She could. She can. She will. Visa regulations have been memorized. Expat forums joined. Google Maps employed to zero in on streets in Pau, Cuenca, Porto and Aveiro.

I've had frank conversations with myself about the realities of living alone in a country with a language with which I will no doubt struggle (barely passing my final high school French exam comes to mind), about the realities of seeing no familiar faces, no familiar routes, no familiar coffee shops, no familiar movie theaters.

But in exchange, new vistas, new faces and infusions of new experiences.

I have a confession. I'm a little tired of the particular trees that surround this house, of these particular walls and problems; is that a leak I hear? The time may have finally come for complete immersion in art and books. In my own work. To work is to avoid dying while living, Rodin believed. I am all for not dying.

A friend will soon go with me to explore potential base camps in Portugal. Coimbra, perhaps, a university town. Or Aveiro, Portugal's Venice. Or maybe further south, the beaches of Algarve. A setting in which I can come to feel at home and from which I can visit the Louvre again. Or the Tate. Or the Rijksmuseum. Explore the Galicia region of Spain. Or places even more far-flung. A place from which I can pull out my wallet to pay for a train ticket instead of a tank of heating oil or new tires.

As we know, wherever we go, we end up with ourselves. Thanks in part to the decade in this wonderful house, this wonderful Connecticut cottage in which I watched my sons grow to manhood, in which I wrote stories that became books, in which I became ever more myself, I am someone I am happy to take along with me to Europe.

Boa viagem.

Swimming: The Silver Bullet

Jan Castle Walker

"There's many a good tune played on an old fiddle."

Proverb

I HAVE A PICTURE OF MYSELF at five, dressed in a bathing suit, standing by the shore in Shalimar, Florida, where we lived when my father was stationed at Eglin AFB as a pilot. It's that image I hold of myself whenever I swim. I see my fit little body with strong thighs, tanned, dripping wet and barefoot. Now you might wonder how I could imagine stuffing the reality of a sixty-seven-year-old woman/grandma into such a tidy little package of a child. But age is a funny bunny. No matter who I must really be, I am still who I was. I don't see myself as old; I see myself as an active person of no age. Swimming helps.

At this writing, I am in my sixth year of masters swimming, and I'd like to tell you a little about the program. My coaches work with over six hundred members of our club — all kinds of people, age eighteen and over. The range is staggering. There is a very dedicated seniors' group, with several members in their nineties. There are fat people, thin people, people with disabilities, triathletes, ex-water-polo players and post-college competitive swimmers, as well as retirees, state workers, college professors, pregnant women and new moms. One of my lane mates, who competes in meets and swims open-water events with the club, lost her lower leg five years ago and swims with a prosthetic.

I thought I was a decent swimmer when I started the program, in spite of the fact that I hadn't trained in many years. Understandably, I was concerned that I might not be strong enough for the required hour of each swim practice, but I'm an optimist, so I went for it. Soon after I began, though, my coach noticed that I was really tired after a hundred-yard set. Fortunately, she was reassuring. "Don't worry about it," she said. "You're just out of shape. Keep swimming. You have to learn how to breathe." I had no idea in the beginning how much more fitness and technical skill I would need to keep up with the program. But day by day, with encouragement and coaching, my abilities and fitness improved.

During the first three months, I swam with Bob, who was then ninety. He began masters swimming at sixty, competed in meets for twenty years and was still working out three times a week. He used swimming for social as well as fitness reasons, and as I was learning to adjust to the program, he was a great lane mate. Bob was a true inspiration and to this day, I think, "I can be here when I'm ninety." Bob's example gave me a personal goal because this was the first time I had ever really thought about how many more years I might have left and what those years ought to look like. Being an active person seemed like a way to achieve my goals of good health and staying involved.

People often dismiss swimming as boring or comment that it's too solitary because it's not a team sport. Why swim those laps? Because for me, exercise is the silver bullet when it comes to health and aging. When I first started the masters program, it was hard to do fifty yards. Now, I swim a mile during each workout. I learned the value of pacing and recovery. Then, with individual medley swims, I had to learn more efficient ways to swim.

The learning is always great, and if you get it, exhausting. It is tiring to break old habits and learn new ones (just like life). And in our case, swimming is not so solitary. The others who swim in my lane are my friends and motivators. We do the sets together, synchronize our timing and feel like a team. We even have time to chat...between sets.

Swimming also makes one more mindful of the body. In the early days, I would think random thoughts during the laps, stuff like how to fix a painting I was working on or what I needed to buy at the grocery store. Over time and with continued coaching, my swimming thoughts focused on how to better move in the water. Now, I think about my body — the position of my hands, for example, or how high my body is in the water. It is the ultimate "be here now" exercise for me. Improvement of technique and being mindful make swimming a worthy and interesting challenge.

That brings me to another point. I am better than when I began. And...I am also six years older now! So my goal is to improve and not just maintain. I've learned that there are many ways to go forward.

Our coach once wrote in a weekly newsletter that swimming is a great way to "offset decrepitude." I laughed when I read that and I love the idea. When I am not on my "A" game and my almost arthritic hands hurt or I trip and fall somewhere or I suffer way too long from a cold, it's easy to succumb to the "I may never get better" mood. So I hang on to the idea that my silver bullet, swimming, will get me better sooner and keep my mind focused on being active and engaged.

Back to that image of myself as a five-year-old... I recently had the great joy of seeing my six-year old granddaughter experience the Gulf waters of Panama City, a beach that is within fifty miles of my five-year-old memories of Shalimar. The warm blue-green water and snow-white sands that day were exactly the same as I remember from my childhood, when the soft winds of the Florida Panhandle caressed me and invited me into the ocean.

My granddaughter and I have been swimming together since she was a toddler. It's one of the ways we have bonded. The day that I watched the surf break over her feet and saw her jump and play in the waves was as thrilling as seeing a filly learn how to run, and it brought me back to my own childhood. As I look back at the five-year-old I was, I remember how utterly amazed I was at the way the waves would endlessly roll up over the white, white sands, leaving a little trace of foam before disappearing. I remember feeling dizzy when the wavy water moved back and forth tickling my ankles and every now and then rushing up my legs. Even when I stood still, my feet sank into the sand.

Even when my granddaughter stood still that day in Panama City, her feet sank into the sand. She got to dance to the same splashy tune that caught me in my youth, and it makes me smile with gratitude to have been able to witness the beginning of her journey as I continue with my own.

Love Is Always a Choice

REV. CLARA Z. ALEXANDER

"For the unlearned, old age is winter; for the learned, it is the season of the harvest."

THE TALMUD

AGING HAS SHOCKED ME. Having been one of the lucky people with a body that did whatever I asked of it, mostly without pain, without broken bones and with ease, I have been very surprised to find that I can now hurt myself doing ordinary things. Muscles get tight just taking a long walk. So odd, since my body has always been flexible. Halfway through knitting a baby blanket, my shoulder hurts, which has never happened before. I've learned to knit for a while then rest my arms, hands and shoulders for a few minutes and then resume, less intensely. And so the learning goes.

How do I cope, adjust and accept the process of living in a changing body? People who are afraid of dying tell me I am lucky to still be alive. Fortunately, I've never been afraid of dying. A frustrating experience in childhood left me with the knowing that being out-of-body is easier than being in one.

And yet I'm still here, learning the losses and gains within this experience of aging.

As I approach seventy, I seek experiences that have nothing to do with age or physical ability. When we can no longer do anything, for example, we can still love. Years ago, a hospice patient confirmed this.

Lucille was in a coma with a diagnosis of

"failure to thrive." I was asked to sit with her, as she was disturbing others in the hospice ward with her loud shrieks and moans. She was curled in a fetal position with legs drawn up and arms and hands clenched to her chest, lying on her side facing me. I sat next to her bed and told her she was safe...that there was nothing more for her to do...to just be. Slowly, she waved her arm, fist clenched. I realized she wanted me to hold her hand, so I wrapped my fingers around her wrist. I could feel her pulse. As I repeated that she was safe, that there was nothing more she needed to do, that all she needed to do was just be, her pulse slowed to a steady rhythm. I suggested that she could forgive others at this time, if there was anyone she needed to forgive, while I kept repeating that she was well cared for and safe. After a pause, I suggested that she could ask for forgiveness if there was someone whose forgiveness she wanted. Later, I offered the sug-gestion that she could forgive herself, knowing that she had done the best she could with the knowledge she'd had. At one point during my time with Lucille, who remained in a coma, she croaked out these words: "Help me" then "Thank you" and, lastly, "I love you." I told her she had just proved my theory that when we can do nothing else we can still love.

One of the nurses told me later that Lucille had released her fetal position and had stopped shrieking, and that she died peacefully.

My time with Lucille was barely an hour and a half, yet as I spoke to her, I felt tremendous love — that I was speaking for the Divine. That glow of love lasted three days and is one of my major spiritual experiences.

People I love will die before me, my health will change, my body will require more maintenance and so on. It is up to me to decide whether the gains outweigh the losses. I can enjoy the freedom to be noticed by strangers or not. Thankfully, men no longer leer or whistle or scare me. I enjoy the courtesy younger men and women offer. Especially the smiles of young ones who come from families who teach respect for elders. I've had white hair since my thirties, which marked me as an elder long before I became one. While with a friend who dyed her hair and was two years older, a young cashier assumed I was my friend's mother. Some thought my daughter (who was born when I was thirty-eight) was my granddaughter. Truthfully, I enjoyed setting them straight! Fearless communication comes with age, I think.

Another freedom is time to do what I want, when I want. Yes, I do some of the things I thought I would when I no longer worked full-time. Yet I'm now amazed at how much I did while raising a child, working full-time and going to school to become an ordained minister. One of the greatest gains for me at this stage of my life is having so much more time to enjoy my husband, my grand-girls, volunteer activities, meeting new people, keeping up with old friends and creating weddings and sacred ceremonies.

Even with the loss of loved ones, my life is rich with treasured memories, delightful new experiences and moments of being of service in these troubled times. Now that I am aging and know I will experience more losses and fewer gains — there is no way to escape them — I find myself thinking more and more about that experience with Lucille. And I know that no matter what happens, I can still love.

Age From here, Is a blessing

Matt Nyman

"Nothing is inherently and invincibly young except spirit. And spirit can enter a human being perhaps better in the quiet of old age and dwell there more undisturbed than in the turmoil of adventure."

George Santayana

Introduction

Age
From here, is a
Blessing.

The rapidly slow passage
Thru
Time and space is
Marked simply by
Cosmic traverses of
Inchoate,
Oblivious masses
Around fiery stars.
All within the
Multitudinous darkness of mostly
Unseen
    Matter
        Force
           Energy.
Scientists tells us we see
A small slice
Of the universe.
Our world.
Is all that is available?
The rest
Unseen.
It is in this framework

Of mostly unknowing
That age confronts
Us. And we ask
"Beyond the orbital rudiments of
Time
What else exists?
And
Why?"

Set up

Age
From here, is a
Blessing.

Stories fill our need to
Flesh out age.
Foundations for remembering, maybe
Even appreciating
The unique emergence of this
Minute.
A cacophony of intersections of
Time
And
Space.
We tell these stories to remember
And grasp that just maybe

Age
From here, is a
Blessing.

The lover with no choice

Age,
From here, is a
Blessing.

"I had always told you
My choice
Not to age.
It's not for me.
Expectations lying
Fallow on
The landscape of
Clichéd talk.
I will not have it."

The adolescent boy's heart was opened to the
world
And the world swallowed.
She had that heart.
Her darkness lent light
Buoying the boy's existence.
In wait, behind darkness and
A visage of intellectual and
Sexual
Energy
There was no blessing in
Age, which
She tossed into a
Destructive arc that had
But
One
Suicidal intersection.

Even now,
20+ years,
The boy waits for the
Call
Of
Explanation
Needed to understand
How age was
A cursed vehicle.
And a reason
Why.

The boy on gravel road

Age
From here, is a
Blessing.

The boy on gravel road
Now looks
Through heavy bifocals.
No mirrors for memories.
Questions of why slide
Smoothly away with
The years.
He settles into the
Warm confines of a
Padded recliner
Poised within the warmth
Of a small room
And buffered from the outside
By wood-fueled heat
And electromagnetic diversions.

There was a man for
The boy on gravel road.
Sturdy. Who once
Carried the boy.
The photos shows
Stance
Arms
Akimbo
And a glare of
Satisfaction.
A new wife.
A farm with New England-styled
Walls of gathered
Field stones
Chiseled by glaciers of
Long ago.
Grasses to cut.
An open barn with
Tools
Scythes
Projects to complete.
And a living to mold.

The boy on gravel road.
Wiry.
With optical needs
Already.
Meshed into and with
The man.
Padding behind with
Room on shoulders
During walks through lengthening

Grass and
Shadows.
The world was full.
Kitchens warmed by
Wood-filled stoves and
Rising loaves of white
Bread.
Meals heavy with buttered
Vegetables
Meat
Dessert.
And the boy on gravel road
Was surrounded
And pulled towards
Center.

The man left in the
Morning
Hours.
Mysteriously vaporized in
A gust of innocuous
Pain
That spread
With no return.
And now the boy on gravel road
Had a cavalcade of
Dark figures
Passing with
Grim
Faces.
Reassuring pats, occasional
Hugs that mingled
With the day's odor of

Diesel
Cut grass and
Manure.

The boy on gravel road
Knew the man would
Return.
So
With long shadows of evening
Pushing him along the
Gravel road
He traveled. And sat.
The shoulders would return.
The warmth encircle him.
The center become fast.

And these dreams, now mixed
With his padded chair respite,
Still echo their loneliness.

Age,
From here, is a
Blessing.

The pleasing girl

Age,
From here, is a
Blessing.

There was no foundation
For
The pleasing girl.
A smattering of warmth

Buffeted by winds of
Indifference. Maybe
Abuse.
And now the dark room and singular
Bed surround her with covers
That try to capture lost
Love.

The mother of
The pleasing girl
Wore her lipstick on
Smoldering cigarettes
And the edges of
Tall high balls.
The father submerged by
Failing business and
Eroding health.
They smile back from padded
Restaurant seats that
Encircle tables laden with
Bottles
Half-filled drinks
Full ashtrays.
Friends raise glasses overhead.
Jocular smiles tempered by
Glazed eyes.

The scurrying kids
Were backdrops.
Four of them.
And the pleasing girl
Attempted to maneuver
Into the parental focal path

That narrowed with time.
Wisps of focus and
Tangents of affection were
Enough,
For the moment, however leaving
Emptiness and uncertainty that
Grew with age and fluctuating
Serotonin.

Eleven was the age of
The pleasing girl.
Rooms dark. The small
House encased with
Blue tobacco clouds
Hushed tones.
Whimpers.
People passed.
The clink of ice on glass and
Menthol smell of
Liniment to clear heads
And soothe bodies.
The pleasing girl was
Penetrated forever by
The shallowness of gasping
Breath and moaning pains.
And when he was gone
The already frayed ropes
Burst.
It was too early and

Age,
From here, is a
Blessing.

Together with other stories

Age,
From here, is a
Blessing.

These stories:
Lovers with no choice
Boys on gravel road
Pleasing girls
And similar others,
Echo the loss of
Age.
Where time did not sit with a
Force to propel us toward the
Quandary of growing old.
Instead
Time sliced
    Skipped
        Bounced
          Glanced
In these stories
Revealing none of the pleasing potential
We grasp within the comfort of tomorrow.

Coda

Age,
From here, is a
Blessing.

Age encompasses us.
Pushing
Shoving

Rude.
And we confront the waning
Of that time with
Incredulity.
Sharing jokes on time's
Torturous linearity.
And in our best we
Embrace impermanence
Change
Disequilibrium.
Riding the swirling eddies
Of seconds
Minutes
Hours
Days
With a frivolity and
Joie de vivre,
Maybe even a sense of purpose,
That shrouds that dark space
Ahead.
It is a blessing?
Isn't it?
This aging.
If not
What
Else

A Lesson in Trust

MF SANBORN

"All the world's a stage,
And all the men and women
merely players:
They have their exits
and their entrances;
And one man in his time
plays many parts,
his act being seven ages."

WILLIAM SHAKESPEARE

ONE OF THE THINGS THAT has surprised me the most about aging is my happiness at living alone. I have always either been in a relationship or been looking for one, always on the elusive search for that "magical other." I thought it was my destiny (turns out it was my addiction) to be partnered with a man: to be wife, girlfriend, significant other. But since my last breakup in the late spring of 2013 at age sixty-eight, I have lived alone. Not partnered, not looking.

I think "boys" took on a Magical/Mysterious aura back in my childhood. I was an only child and went to Catholic schools, where girls and boys were in separate classrooms; like if we were mixed, something dreadful might happen. From there I went to an all-girls' high school and then a girls' junior college. So I never had any kind of a normal experience with the opposite sex, other than with cousins or neighborhood boys. Being shy didn't help, either.

But I was curious. I wanted to know one of those creatures. As a teenager, I wanted to attract one and, according to the teen magazines I read, I could. I was blonde, thin, attractive: perfect bait. And though my heart longed for the deeply poetic, motorcycle-riding, slightly dangerous boy from the local prep school, I caught the attention of a lifeguard at the beach, with a little help from a white bikini.

It was a predictable choice of a husband for a nineteen-year-old. He was tall, handsome, had won the scholar/athlete award in his high school graduation class and had the same middle-class background as my own. Mostly, the thing that got me (aside from his tan and big smile) was that he had a plan (I did not), and he invited me to come along. His plan was to apply for Navy flight training after he graduated from college. The Navy, though, was just a means to an end. He wanted to make the big money, as an airline pilot. It was a crazy time to think about entering the military, the Vietnam War was ramping up and he might well have to go. It turned out that he didn't. He lucked out with two Mediterranean deployments. But we had many friends who did end up in Vietnam and some who died.

During his training, I began to feel resentful that he was learning to fly jets in the Navy and was excited about his life, while I, a pampered only child, was washing his clothes, cooking his meals from a Betty Crocker cookbook and tiptoeing around our tiny rented house when he studied. At the Officers' Club, we young wives were gathered together and told by a senior officer how special our husbands were: the best of the best, the cream of the crop and every other cliche of excellence. Our men were bright, brave and could die at any moment. So our responsibility was to take care of them and not do anything to cause them stress, because they could die or kill someone else. And that, the senior officer implied, would be our fault.

My husband did eventually get hired by an airline. Unfortunately, he discovered that it was like being a glorified bus driver. Fortunately, he was part of a mass layoff and ended up back in the Navy, teaching. It was during that time that he was introduced to a profession that matched his fierce ambition.

He came home one day and said, "I saw this man in an office just staring at a screen for hours on end. It must be fascinating, whatever it is he's doing." The man became his mentor and when it was time for him to leave the Navy, he landed a job at E.F. Hutton and became one of those legendary, fearless traders of the seventies who ordered Ferrari cocktails at lunch like they were ordering sandwiches from the deli. From five years as a Navy fighter pilot, he became a Wall Street rich guy at the hottest game in town: commodities trading. Years later, I watched *Top Gun* and *Wolf of Wall Street* and knew that I had lived that life.

Thanks to his skill at trading, we had a six-thousand-square-foot home with swimming pool and tennis court, not to mention expensive cars: Jaguar, Ferrari, Porsche. I drove a Mercedes SL convertible, anthracite gray with saddle interior. Apart from the house in the suburbs, we had an apartment in New York, front-row tickets to any Broadway show we wanted and a penthouse condo in Florida. Our two sons were in the local private grammar school, which would insure their admittance to a good prep school. I was living the American Dream, but I was crying every day. I felt empty and sad: I had no real intimacy with my husband, and my children were acting out.

I began to keep a journal, to try to figure out my life. The first words I wrote on Valentine's Day 1979 were "I am not happy." I was 33.

Thus began my Renaissance. I went back to college, finally pursuing my own growing interests in psychology, philosophy, literature and photography. I was good at photography, made some interesting images, even won some awards. Three years later I had an invitation from a master photographer in New Mexico. I traveled to meet him and took the biggest leap of my life, on my own, deciding to move from Cambridge to Santa Fe to be his apprentice. I was finally going for something that was mine, but it meant leaving my sons who were in prep school, my parents, my friends and everything familiar for a leap of faith into the Wild West. My husband and I had separated a few years earlier, though we had remained close and co-parented our sons.

I had moved to find myself and to find work that was meaningful, but I soon found myself in another relationship, with a man who was to have a profound impact on my life.

He was a young friend of my mentor (almost five years younger than my then-age of thirty-nine), a brilliant up-and-coming artist in Santa Fe's corral of creative painters. He was a renegade, rebellious, draft-dodging hippie and, in his own words, a "junkyard dog" who looked like a movie star. He was fascinating and a bit dark and dangerous (you only had to listen to him laugh) and, at the same time, infectious and diabolical. He was the archetypal bad boy: sexy, passionate, a lightning strike! He was driven too, like my husband had been, but in a different direction: art.

I was captivated and, it turns out, so was he. He was the answer to my prayer, the most fun I'd ever had in my life, and he put me on the kind of path-with-the-heart that Joseph Campbell wrote about. He put clay into my hands and taught me how to pinch and fire a pot. We built a studio in the backyard made from four thousand adobes bricks, the same building I live in today. It took us nine months to build, and we called it our baby. On lawn chairs in the yard at night, we watched the stars swirl by. We adopted a husky named Big Boy, who became our trusted companion for the next fifteen years. In addition to our home in Santa Fe, we bought an Airstream, which we drove through Big Bend, Death Valley and the Pinacates Peaks in upper Baja. We called our traveling vessel *The Argo*, after Jason's fabled ship. We would sit in the greenhouse of our home in the mornings, drinking coffee, reading Dante's *Divine Comedy* aloud to each other and laugh that others were hurrying off to their nine-to-five jobs. Too much hubris. We were ripe for a fall.

He was The Artist, so of course he had a dark side: the raging, misunderstood "next-Picasso" who was ignored by the world. Infuriated, he'd rant in clouds of marijuana smoke. He was included in art shows but cursed about not being taken seriously. We lived mostly on my money, which I shared but kept control of, a potentially bad situation. As in all fairy tales, there was the fatal flaw.

With him as The Artist, I became The Housewife again (now that's a combination doomed to fail!), even as I struggled to have my creative life in clay and painting. No longer Pluto and Persephone, we fell into the mundane world of who's going to take out the garbage and why can't you remember to lock the house when you go out.

I think we finally ended because I quit trying to make it work. We were always at the edge of disaster in the later years. Then, somehow, I'd make it all better and save us at the last minute. We were together most of fifteen years, though, and it was agonizing to split. It took two years before we managed to keep our distance. Our differences, which had at first drawn us together, eventually drove us apart.

The split did not stop me from wanting another relationship, though. I wanted more of what we had, but better. Instead of focusing on why I had moved to New Mexico, my own work, I kept trying to find Him again. That's where my needle got stuck, on "Find Him Again."

Six more relationships followed in the next dozen years, from the industrialist to the yoga spiritualist, until three and a half years ago when I said, "Enough!" I realized that all the red flags that I had ignored in the beginning were not going to get fixed. Nothing was going to change. I had once again stepped into a relationship that wasn't right for me, just to be in one. It had been six years and I was feeling like I was being pulled into a black hole. "We're going to spin in this circle until the end of time," I admitted to myself. And then a wise person said to me, "You can leave, you know." And I did.

I'm still involved in many non-male relationships. I have wonderful, longtime friends, near and far, most of them women, and with them I laugh, talk deep and break bread. These friendships are soul-satisfying to me. Living alone does not mean isolation.

This single change of attitude, of habit, of that feeling that I need to have another person in my life to feel complete, has changed everything. I can now be alone because I trust myself to take care of me. My lesson to learn was that I couldn't be in an intimate relationship without trust, and I first had to trust myself. I've begun that process. I enjoy my own company, I love my life and I'm figuring out how to take care of myself financially with work that's meaningful to me. As I use my strengths, I'm gaining strength. I'm stronger, not weaker and more vulnerable, even at this pretty ripe age. Turns out, *I* am the magical other.

These past few years have brought amazing opportunities. Being able to choose what I want to do and with whom, where I want to place my attention. Having the freedom to visit family and friends who live in other parts of the country. Being more committed to my spiritual practice of yoga and meditation. Binge-watching *Breaking Bad* or turning off the television for days at a time. I can say "yes" in a single moment without having to check with anyone. I don't criticize my body for not being perfect. In fact, I praise it for still getting me up a several-thousand-foot climb in the mountains and for allowing me to sit comfortably on the floor, legs folded under me. Thank you, body! Thank you, heart, limbs, lungs! I get to choose the creative projects I want to be engaged in and enthused about. I spend time every day in the natural beauty of New Mexico, constantly flabbergasted by the sky or the colors or the storms. I can stop whatever I'm doing to take a photograph, or dance across the room, or sit down to pray.

I was raised in a time when coupling and children was what one did. I knew then that that would be my life. I was afraid to face life alone, and the child in me loomed large long after she should have been put to bed. I wanted to share the responsibility of living life, emotionally and financially. I never felt prepared to live on my own. But now that I'm seventy-one and on my own, at a time when many others my age are winding down, I'm revving my engines, I'm accomplishing things I wasn't able to when I was younger. Meeting goals, taking more risks.

Aging doesn't mean you're not alive. I find that I can figure it out; I do have resources. I have learned I'm stronger than I thought, and that I can stand on my own and face what comes. And I have learned that I'm not ever really alone. I have family and fabulous friends who love and support me through all of the triumphs and low points. Ironically, I'm the best-suited I have ever been for a relationship. And though I'm not opposed to one, I'm not waiting for it, either. I'm grateful for exactly what I have. I live now to experience my own awakening into an awareness beyond self. I lean into life, curious and unafraid.

Red Hot Mama Until the End!

SUSAN SWIDERSKI

"It's paradoxical that the idea of living a long life appeals to everyone, but the idea of getting old doesn't appeal to anyone."

ANDY ROONEY

BACK IN THE 1940s, when my mother was in the process of forcibly evicting me from the cozy comfort of her womb, her glasses were taken away from her in the delivery room. After the doctor finished yanking me out with forceps, she squinted at me and afterward told my father they had a beautiful baby boy with curly black hair and a really long *hoojie*. (Her word, not mine!) Needless to say, my severely myopic mother insisted they'd brought in the wrong baby when they wheeled me into her room later that day. I mean, there I was — *ta-DA!* — bald as a cue ball, with a smashed nose and two black eyes and completely devoid of a *hoojie* of any length whatsoever. So much for naming me Ian.

Fortunately, they quickly reconciled themselves to the fact that they had a daughter and that I was, indeed, their kid. They also laughed about that day more times than I can count. But you know, no matter how different your entrance into this world may have been from mine, the birth of every single person on this planet has one irrefutable thing in common, and it doesn't have a thing to do with hair color or the presence or absence of any specific body parts: At that singular and magnificent moment of birth, when our mamas squeeze us out into the cold world, red-faced, kicking and screaming, that, my friend, is the youngest we will ever be. It's all downhill from there.

Remember what it was like to be a child? We didn't fully appreciate our youthfulness, and we foolishly urged time to pass more quickly because we could hardly wait to become one of the big kids so we could enjoy big-kid privileges and do big-kid things. Then we ached to be teenagers, to go on our first date, share our first kiss, drive a car, fall in love, get married, raise a family.

Right about the time we started squeezing out our own children, something nefarious started happening. Our long-ago wish suddenly came true, and no matter how hard we tried to hang onto it and savor it, time really was moving faster and our children were growing up much too quickly. Before we knew what hit us, our nest was empty again and we were looking skyward, wondering where all the years went.

Then, oh boy, that's when things really got crazy. I'm telling you, once we go on Social Security and Medicare, I'm convinced we senior citizens no longer get our full allotment of twenty-four hours in a day. I kid you not. The hands on my office clock have been spinning so fast, I don't even need a fan in here anymore.

So what happened? When, exactly, did I go from being a fairly attractive, hip young woman to being an old bag with arthritic hips? I honestly don't know. To tell the truth, sometimes I forget how old I am. I mean, no matter how old you are on the outside, don't you still feel young on the inside? No matter what that lying mirror tries to tell you, don't you still feel the same? Don't you still look at the world through the same eyes, smell the roses with the same nose and laugh with the same sense of humor?

For me, the first wake-up call that I might possibly be getting old came about a decade ago, when our local newspaper described a crime victim as being elderly...and that poor gal was several years younger than I was at the time. How insulting! I mean, how could *she* possibly be elderly when I was still *young*, dammit?

Even so, just in case that article writer was right, I decided there and then not to run for re-election to a statewide position I was holding at the time. Instead, I decided to put more energy into doing some of the things I wanted to do and to pursuing some of the dreams I'd put on hold for way too long. Bottom line, before I was pushing up daisies, I wanted to spend more time appreciating them. So I started writing again. Since then, I've had several articles and stories published, I've written and published a novel and I've started writing a blog. Yeah, okay, so I'm still old, but I've never been happier.

I got another dose of reality when I tried to show one of my granddaughters how to jump rope the way I did as a young girl. I convinced her and my son to spin the rope, so I could demonstrate the fine art of jumping in. Remember doing that? Well, Chloe and my son got the rope to spinning in a nice steady rhythm, while I stood there, biding my time until I could pick the perfect moment to jump in...just like I used to do. Nailed it, too! Pretty as a picture, I jumped on into that spinning rope and started skipping it...just like I used to do. It felt great! For a few beautiful moments, I felt as graceful and light on my feet as a ten-year-old ballerina. But then, zip-a-dee-doo-dah, my feet went out from under me and the next thing I knew, my keister hit the driveway like a one-ton sack of potatoes. I thought it was absolutely hilarious, but everybody else? Not so much. My husband, son, daughter-in-law and grandchildren were absolutely horrified. They hovered over me as though I were some kind of fragile invalid, instead of the youthful, fun-loving grandmother I imagined myself to be. No matter how I saw myself and how I felt on the inside, they saw me as an old lady who had no business trying to jump rope.

Then a friend of ours died. At the cemetery, a number of chairs were set up at the grave-side, but did I sit in one of them? Nope. Instead, I stood with my husband, shifting my weight from one aching foot to the other, while rubbing my sore back. Then it hit me upside the head. *Bam!* Those chairs had been set up as a courtesy for the older women in attendance, and a quick look around told me I *was* one of those older women. When I realized that, it was all I could do to keep from laughing out loud at my own idiocy. When we got home, I called my best friend and we shared a laugh over those darned chairs and what they meant. Then we agreed that if she and I go somewhere together when we're in our nineties, we're probably still going to stand politely on the sidelines, so the older ladies can use the chairs...because we don't *see* ourselves as old.

Not long ago, my six-year-old granddaughter, Kymber, asked me how old I was. When I told her, she looked at me with wide eyes and said in a very somber tone of voice, "You're going to die."

As you can imagine, that kinda caught me by surprise. But in spite of her parents' mortification and protests, I managed to smile at her and said, "Yes, sweetie, but not today." Reassured, she went back to playing with her brothers and sister. Luckily, fate didn't make a liar out of me that day.

Yes, I get it. I *am* old and I *am* gonna die. But what matters is that I'm still here today and plan to be here for as many more days as life grants me. I look at pictures of myself from long ago and see someone with a shiny, smiling face and a fairly smoking hot body, and I find it hard to remember that I don't look like that anymore. At some point, I think we all reach the day where we catch sight of our reflection in the mirror and see the face of a parent or, God help us, a grandparent, looking back at us. For now, I prefer to believe our house is haunted. On those rare occasions when I attempt to look in the mirror, some terribly rude, fat old lady ghost jumps right in front of me, so I can't see myself. Seeing that old bat in the mirror is as much of a shock as my mother must have felt when the nurse gave me to her instead of the beautiful baby boy she expected to see. No way that could be *my* baby, she thought. No way that could be *me*, says I. Sure, that may be the person the world sees when it looks at me, but it isn't the real *me*. Nuh-uh. The real me is still a daredevil with boundless energy, a smart-ass sense of humor and, yes, a fairly smoking hot body.

It's a sobering thought when we realize how far the road stretches behind us and how little road remains ahead. But that doesn't mean we shouldn't keep going, that we shouldn't continue to enjoy the trip to the very end. Life is an ongoing project from start to finish, and we should never give up on it before it gives up on us. I'm still very young at heart. Yeah, the rest of me is considerably older and showing signs of wear and tear, but that's okay. We've got to go with the flow and do our best to find humor in every situation, and we've got to appreciate every blessing that comes our way. Currently, I'm working on another book. Matter of fact, it's the first book of a trilogy. Yeah...what can I say? I'm still a daredevil and a bit of a gambler. So what if I don't live long enough to finish it? It doesn't matter. As long as I am able, I'm still going to try. And I'm going to enjoy doing it every step of the way.

Yep, my go-go boots went-went a long time ago, and those sexy stilettos I used to wear will never find their way back onto my tired old feet. Instead, they sit silently in my closet, testaments to the past. And I often wave to them fondly while putting on my sensible old lady shoes. But it's all good. I've had a good life, and my head and heart are filled with many happy memories. My husband and I are still together after all these years, and we're sharing these so-called golden years together with an irreverent sense of humor and a determination to enjoy whatever time we have left.

And here's the kicker. We've decided to be cremated, so do you know what that means? For one last time, this sassy old broad, this red hot mama, will be going out in a blaze of glory...and with a truly smoking hot body!

Ode to Old Age

I found a hair there under my chin,
And I yanked that sucker out,
But wouldn't you know, the very next day,
Two more began to sprout.
I don't know what's happening;
It's a perplexing change of pace.
My arms and legs are going bald,
But I have to shave my face.

It's such a rotten travesty;
My tummy once was flat.
But now my hourglass is mostly ass,
And my waist has turned to fat.
My body's slowly sagging,
And I don't look so hot;
If a man wants to ogle my bosom now,
I'm afraid he'll have to squat.

But that's okay, 'cause I'm still here,
Of life I'm still a part.
So what if when I bend or stretch,
I leak a little fart?
I've lots of life and love in store,
Though I'm not young and shiny;
If ya wanna know the truth,
Old age can kiss my heinie.

Aging Isn't a Choice. Living Is.

KAREN HELENE WALKER

"The old-fashioned way of looking at aging is that you're born, you peak at midlife and then you decline into decrepitude. The way to really look at it is, even if your body is declining, even if you're sick, your spirit, your heart is on an upward trajectory, always growing and evolving."

JANE FONDA

A HEART BEGINS TICKING about sixteen days after the egg is fertilized in the uterus. That means our biological clock starts nine months before we are born. But we usually don't start thinking about it until we have children... or until we start losing parents. That's what happened for me. The first time I really got that my time here on Earth wasn't infinite was when I began caring for both my dad and mother-in-law during the last years of their lives. I saw how their hearing and eyesight diminished, how hard it was for them to give up driving, to give up their home and eventually to give up their independence, and I realized that some day I'd be at that stage of life when those sorts of losses would begin to occur for me. When I might not be able to do the things I love. When I would begin losing even more loved ones.

I'm only a few years away from seventy and I am enjoying myself more than I ever thought possible. I take tap dance lessons — something I did as a child and gave up for reasons that don't matter anymore. I perform at retirement communities in a duo called Sugartime; we sing and dance to old standards and Broadway hits, as well as to country and pop tunes. I try not to think about how much longer I'll be able to do these things, but there are two women in my tap class who are in their late eighties, so I keep my fingers crossed.

The whole idea of aging seems cruel to me. We work hard our whole lives, look forward to retirement, then when we get there, boom, we reach the stage of diminishing returns. Well, it may be cruel, but it is the reality of the life cycle and I'm working on accepting it. Acceptance, for me, means that one day I won't be here anymore. Let me be blunt: That means I'm going to die.

I haven't really thought about my own death much. I'm not aware of any fear around dying, perhaps because I have a strong spiritual foundation and believe that I'll be going someplace wonderful when I pass. But when I cared for my dad and mother-in-law, I began to fear aging. I don't want to lose my ability to think clearly. I need to be able to communicate, verbally and in writing. I don't ever want to have to stop singing and dancing. And I can't even imagine losing a friend to illness or death.

But we have no control over what we want or over the reality of life. Some or all of those things may, indeed, happen to me. The key is for me to learn to handle whatever happens with dignity and grace. To keep finding ways to have meaning in my life even when I must stop doing what gives my life meaning now.

Our biological clocks keep ticking as long as they are meant to, then they stop. I have no idea when I'm going to die. None of us does, unless we have been diagnosed with a terminal illness and have been given an approximate timeline. Yet I've heard many stories of people not buying into those prognoses and living much longer than originally predicted. So, truly, we can't know when we will die.

More importantly for me, the question has become how will I live? I want to live what I call "full-tilt boogie", using every moment wisely. Doing things I love. Things that give me moments of joy. Things that are deeply satisfying. Things that perhaps make a difference in someone else's life. I'm doing that some of the time, but I waste way too much time and the clock is running down.

The biggest challenge I face as I age is physical. I've not taken good enough care of my body and so my muscles are weaker than they should be. I've had gall bladder surgery, a hysterectomy, a caesarian section, rotator cuff repair, arthroscopy, a fractured ankle, a heart ablation, yada yada yada. They've all taken their toll on my body. Exercising doesn't come easily. Dance, yes. Exercise, no. Weights? Forget it. I observe older friends having to use walkers and canes and still falling. I don't want to be that person. So I did something I said I'd never do. I joined a gym. I am, indeed, doing weights and water aerobics in order to help my body become as healthy as possible. And walking on days I'm not at the gym.

Yet even as I strive to become physically stronger, it is to the spiritual world that I turn more and more. Because unless my mind is completely gone, no matter what is occurring physically, I can find strength in my spirituality.

It's a bit ironic that as I move closer to leaving my body for good, I'm only just beginning to actually be "in" it. And to understand just what it's done for me, how it's taken care of me, how it's tried to protect me. Because of traumatic events in my childhood, I learned to disassociate, to not feel bodily sensations connected to emotional upsets. Now I'm learning to stay fully here in the present moment and to have emotional reactions and responses in real time.

The disconnection from my body and my emotions kept me disconnected as well from what I call Spirit, that universal energy that unites everyone and everything. I know some don't believe in God or a Higher Power or whatever one may choose to call it, but my belief in something greater than myself is what sustains me and keeps me from despair. My task now is to connect to Spirit whenever and wherever possible, not just in ten-minute chunks of meditation time. I do this when I walk in nature. It happens sometimes when I'm singing and really connect with the lyrics and melody. Or when someone tells me I've touched them in some way. Oftentimes, it happens when I'm writing. Spirit is all around me. I just have to be awake enough to notice.

And as the aging process progresses and things in my life diminish, I will continue to find ways to connect with Spirit for as long as I am here. Because for me, nothing is diminished in the Spirit world. It is all Light and, I believe, so are we. I just need to remember that.

About the Authors

REV. CLARA ALEXANDER is an ordained New Thought minister who creates and performs sacred ceremonies, including unique weddings, funerals, memorial services, baby blessings and house blessings. She is also a popular speaker, inspiring groups with her talks on how we cling to our grudges, how we overuse the phrase "I'm sorry" and how we can live the life we love.

WENDY BROWN recently retired from a career in wildlife biology, where she studied sandhill cranes and whooping cranes as they migrated from Idaho to New Mexico. Wendy eventually found a permanent home in Albuquerque, where she and her husband enjoy the sounds of sandhill cranes from their deck.

Since retiring from state government in 2014, VALERIE CAPPS has bypassed the porch rocking chair to pursue her life-long passion for writing, thereby proving that in today's world, life *can* begin again at 65! Valerie lives in Nashville with her husband and their spoiled-rotten Welsh Corgi. www.amazon.com/Valerie-Capps/e/B016VD9V72

MARY W. CLARK retired from her law practice in 2007 and transferred her observation and composition skills to travel writing. She is currently working on a book about her father's World War II experience flying "the Hump" from India to China over the Himalayas. Mary lives in Paris, Texas. www.maryclarktraveler.com

FRAN FISCHER: "I was born at a very young age and that happened 82 years ago, so I don't remember much about it. I've crammed as much living into my life as possible, and I'm not through yet. I've traveled extensively and I even flew in the same zero-gravity plane that the astronauts trained in. I live in California with my first (and only) husband, and we celebrated our 62nd anniversary this year."

PAT GARCIA (Patricia Anne Pierce-Garcia Schaack) is an American expatriate living in Europe. An accomplished musician as well as a writer, she has been writing (and reading) since childhood.

MARK DAVID GERSON is the author of more than a dozen books, including critically acclaimed titles for writers, award-winning fiction and compelling memoirs. Known as "The Birthing Your Book Guru," Mark David works with an international roster of clients as coach and consultant, helping them get their stories onto the page and into the world with ease. www.markdavidgerson.com

HOLLY DEUEL GILSTER plays "make believe" for a living. In other words, she is a professional actress and musician. Holly also loves painting with words as an accomplished poet, an award-winning short-story writer and a book-reviewer for *The Orff Echo*.

AARON GORDON is a retired social sciences community college professor. He and his wife, Ellie, have been married for 65 years and have three children and grandchildren.

ELLIE GORDON is a retired public school teacher who spent the best 20 years of her life in the classroom. A Chicago native, she now lives in New Mexico.

KARLA "ROSIE" HARPER recently retired from teaching elementary school, freeing her to return to her early love of dancing. Today, when not helping out with her grandchildren, Rosie is taking dance lessons, spinning on a dance floor or performing in senior centers and retirement communities with Albuquerque's Sugartime, as singer as well as dancer.

LINDA HOYE is the author of *Two Hearts: An Adoptee's Journey Through Grief to Gratitude*, available through major online retailers. A native of Saskatchewan, Linda currently lives in British Columbia (by way of Washington State) with her husband and doted-upon Yorkshire Terrier. www.lindahoye.com

E.V. Legters hasn't so much retired as she has exchanged one life for another — from rewarding years with career and children (while pursuing the arts on the fly) to a life with the arts at its center. She is the author of *Vanishing Point* and *Connected Underneath* and is currently hard at work on her third novel. www.evlegters.com

LD Masterson lived on both coasts before becoming landlocked in Ohio. After twenty years managing computers for the American Red Cross, she now divides her time between writing, volunteer work and enjoying her grandchildren. Her short stories have been published in several magazines and anthologies, and she is currently working on a new novel. www.ldmasterson.com

Kathleen Messmer not only runs a film-production company with offices in the UK and the US, she is an avid photographer and wildlife advocate. In the unlikely event that she ever retires, Kathleen plans to live on a ranch with draft horses and pygmy goats and vineyards and fruit orchards, somewhere near the water. Oh, and a cowboy...maybe. www.kathleenmessmer.com

Karen Norstad has worked as cashier/gift wrapper, secretary, boutique seamstress, administrative assistant, manager of employee stock options, executive assistant and budget analyst.

Now retired, Karen's life revolves around lounging about, wearing PJs until four in the afternoon, obsessing over the news, reading, fusing and slumping glass, practicing piano, keeping a small balcony garden and cooking.

MATT NYMAN's nonlinear career path has included working in the geological sciences, teaching high school, stay-at-home parenting and, currently, training tomorrow's teachers. Poetry frequently resides near the surface of his existence, occasionally erupting onto paper.

JILL PLAMAN was born and began aging in Milwaukee, but she has lived and worked in Albuquerque since 1977. She holds a BS from the University of Wisconsin-Milwaukee and an MSW from the University of Minnesota. Her special interests are travel, international folk dancing, reading, hiking and spending time with family and friends.

MAUREEN POLIKOFF is a clinical social worker/ therapist who has always pursued many other creative endeavors, including painting, playing music and, now, writing. A Connecticut native, she lives in New Mexico with her husband, Michael.

MF SANBORN left Boston 33 years ago to apprentice with photographer Walter Chappell in Santa Fe. Still in love with the beauty of the Southwest, she photographs, writes, hikes, travels, teaches yoga and meditation, makes soups on Sundays, and dreams of the ocean and whales.

PATRICIA STOLTEY is the author of four mystery novels. The most recent is *Wishing Caswell Dead*. She lives in Northern Colorado with Sassy Dog, Katie Cat and her husband, Bill. www.patriciastolteybooks.com

SUSAN SWIDERSKI grew up in Dundalk, Maryland, where everybody calls everybody hon and eating steamed crabs is a sacrament. Although she's happy in her adopted Georgia, part of her heart still lingers on the shores of Chesapeake Bay, explaining the setting for her novel, *Hot Flashes and Cold Lemonade*. Susan is currently working on a trilogy, proof that this old gal is still a pathological optimist. www.susan-swiderski.blogspot.com

JAN CASTLE WALKER is a retired teacher and an active artist. She lives in Davis, California with her husband, Mack. www.jancastlewalker.com

KAREN HELENE WALKER is a novelist, memoirist and essayist and the author of *The Wishing Steps* and *Following the Whispers*. When not writing, Karen is tap dancing, folk dancing or performing with the musical group Sugartime at retirement communities. Karen is currently working on her second memoir. www.karenfollowingthewhispers.blogspot.com

June 2018

I read Linda's + a few other stories night after — the very night — infact I got back from Omega's workshop Women writing to change the world —

And I really — I can do this! Can be a published writer.

insta: linda leszczuk

Made in the USA
Middletown, DE
08 May 2018